A COLLECTION OF COLUMNS

RICK T. RAE

authorHOUSE

AuthorHouse™
1663 Liberty Drive
Bloomington, IN 47403
www.authorhouse.com
Phone: 833-262-8899

Published by AuthorHouse 02/03/2023

ISBN: 978-1-6655-7311-5 (sc)
ISBN: 978-1-6655-7312-2 (e)

Library of Congress Control Number: 2022918776

Print information available on the last page.

This book is Dedicated to the current and former employees of the following newspapers. Some of these publications no longer exist, Reflecting the decline of the business that I toiled in for over nearly half a century. Those that remain are just shadows of their former selves as reflected in these words from Bob Dylan's Masters of War....

And I hope you die, and your death will come soon
I'll follow your casket in the pale afternoon
And I will watch as you lay in your deathbed
And I'll stay over your tomb till I'm sure that you're dead
Dylan – Masters of War

The Hamilton (Ont) Spectator
The Winnipeg (Man) Tribune (deceased)
The Windsor (Ont) Star
The Oakland (MI) Press
The Hamilton (OH) Journal News (deceased)
The Sevierville (TN) Mountain Press
The Light Newspapers, LaJolla, (CA)
Southern Farm Publications Raleigh, (NC)
The Martinsburg (WV) Morning Journal
The Irwin (PA) Standard Observer (deceased)
The Rockdale (GA) Citizen
The Newton GA) Citizen
The Gwinnett (GA) Daily Post

By Rick T. Rae
Cover design by Kit Rae

CONTENTS

FOREWORD

My first book was published in August, 2012. It covered the highlights of my publishing career from 1966 through 2010, 44 years of managing newspaper operations.

After retiring from newspapers in 2006, my wife and I bought a company that produced color comic sections for Sunday newspapers in the southeastern USA, called Continental Features.

We ran that company as a division of Rae Media Services, a corporation we formed to oversee some consulting business as well as the comics operation. As things developed, I continued to write and contributed columns to some of my newspaper clients that were published from time to time. Readers of my stuff would often comment that I ought to package these columns and publish them together in book form.

At the end of 2018, we shut down our corporation after I suffered a stroke and could not continue, but the urge to write continued on and electronic communications enabled me to contribute my musings to a much smaller audience as traditional newspaper distribution continued to decline.

Friends and former colleagues suggested I package my columns together in book form, so I sat down at age 83 to produce this book. It will never be a best seller but I hope you enjoy it.

Respectfully,

Rick T. Rae
Loganville, Georgia
September, 2022

I came to Georgia in 1996 and a few years later began to write a series of columns in the Rockdale Citizen and Gwinnett Daily Post about various cars I had owned. Here is the first of these from March 2003.

CHAPTER ONE

MY MODEL A

DISCOVERY IN A FARMER'S FIELD

Last month, I acquired a new car, bringing the total number of cars I have owned in my lifetime to 56. If that seems excessive, you have to understand that I love automobiles.

For a time, I collected the real thing, When my stable got up to five I quickly realized I did not have the funds to continue enjoying such a hobby. Collectible cars can be good investments, but people usually lose more than they gain on such ventures. An older car is only worth what someone is willing to pay for it at a specific time, and it seems I always found the wrong time to buy and the wrong time to sell.

As visitors to my office in Conyers, Georgia understand, my love of cars is on display along one wall. Glass shelves contain about 60 model cars that I have scratch-built or fashioned from kits over the years. This is much less satisfying than owning the real thing, but it protects my marriage, as my wife doesn't share my enthusiasm for cars.

My latest ride is a 2003 Mitsubishi Spyder, replacing the Mustang Cobra convertible I had been driving. While not quite as quick as the Cobra, it is a treat to drive, and we'll work on waking the engine up a bit with some planned modifications.

My first car was a 1931 Ford Model A that I rescued from a field in southern Ontario during summer vacation after my first year of high school. My summer job was working in a Texaco service station, so that gave me a place to bring it back to life.

The rusted floorboards were replaced with a sheet of plywood that I cut to fit, and some old draperies that my mother wanted to throw out replaced the headliner that had rotted away while it sat in the field. The motor eventually seized, and I got my first taste of rebuilding an engine on that venerable four-cylinder Ford. I ran into a few problems, but the guy I worked for helped me out from time to time and thanks to Albert, my Buddy Ray's father, assistance. By the time school began, I had my own mode of transportation up and running again.

One day I decided to add fog lamps to the car and was drilling a hole in the dashboard to mount the switch when my service station boss pulled the plug on the drill. *"What the h--- do you think you're doing!"* he yelled.

What I hadn't considered was that on a Model A the gas tank is up front under the cowl, and the dash is a thin sheet of metal running in front of the tank. A hot drill spinning into a full tank of gas could have made for an interesting time had my boss not intervened.

The fall semester saw me running my Model A in red lead primer as I spent the evenings leading in rust spots and wet sanding in preparation for painting. Henry Ford once said, *"The Model A can be delivered in any color you want as long as it is black."* I didn't want black, so just before Christmas I spent the weekend applying several coats of "refrigerator white" to my old Ford.

As spring came, my "ice box white" Model A was the talk of the school and seemed to attract members of the opposite sex. Nowadays, I guess that would be called a "chick magnet."

With a top speed of 52 mph, I wasn't in much danger of getting caught speeding, and I put several thousand miles on it before it was time to move on to faster, more comfortable transportation.

Rick Rae is publisher of the Citizen and president of Post-Citizen Media Inc.

CHAPTER TWO

MORE ON CARS I'VE OWNED

A FOLLOW UP ON THE MODEL A

by Rick Rae

In a previous column I talked about my first car that was a 1931 Ford Model A. I appreciate the comments from readers who took the time to e-mail and write me citing similar bouts of nostalgia about their early Fords. One more comment on the Model A before I move on.

Henry Ford was very slow to make changes on his automobiles, Both General Motors and Chrysler had changed from mechanical to hydraulic brakes in the early '30's but Henry stuck with mechanical brakes until two or three years after the other manufacturers.

My Model A had mechanical brakes. It was a simple arrangement with the brake pedal activating a rod that was attached using a clevis to another rod running to the rear of the car; connected to the brake shoes. When pushed, the brake pedal moved this series of rods to activate the shoes against the brake drums.

One night I was double dating with my friend John. I had picked up my date and we were on the way to pick up John when I came to an intersection, pushed on the brakes and nothing happened! The pedal went to the floor. I quickly geared down, which was no mean feat in a Model A as the transmission wasn't synchronized for first gear... and rolled it to a stop against a curb. Crawling under the car, I found that the cotter pin, holding the clevis to the brake rod had fallen out and disconnected things.

Slightly late getting to John's house, I went to the door and found him anxiously waiting. His mother came to the door and I quickly asked her if she had a safety pin. She went down the hall and returned with a pin and handed it to me. They then watched in amazement as I crawled under the car and put my brakes back together with that pin. I think I ran the car that way for a couple of weeks afterward.

About a year later I finally tired of a top speed of 52 miles per hour and decided to sell my 'A' and upgrade. I negotiated a deal with a classmate, sold it for $200 and then bought a 1947

Pontiac coupe for $150. It didn't take long for me to remove all the chrome trim, fill in the holes, add a set of wide whitewalls, moon wheel discs and paint it all black. Although speedier than the old Ford, it had an in-line six-cylinder engine, that didn't measure up to some of my friends with V8's but it was an improvement for me.

That old six-cylinder engine proved to be almost indestructible, but I tried my best to blow it up.

One of my many driving faults was following too closely. It took several lessons to cure me of that habit. The first came when I was following a car that slammed on the brakes at a caution light. I locked up mine and crumpled the bumper, front fenders and grille on my newly painted Pontiac.

Once I paid for the repairs on the 1955 Chrysler I ran into, I had no money left to repair my own car. (The owner was kind enough not to report the collision to the authorities). I limped my car home with steam coming out from what was left of my radiator and parked it.

Saturday was a cold one even for Canadian winters with temperatures in the low teens. That gave me an idea. With freezing fingers, I took off the bent bumper, unbolted the damaged grille and radiator from the car, disconnected all the hoses and banged out the fenders with a hammer.

I found that I could drive that old six-cylinder without the radiator in an air-cooled mode for about 20 minutes before it would begin to overheat and start to miss. Since my school was just a 10-minute drive from my house, I took to driving to and from school that winter with an air-cooled Pontiac.

One day, I foolishly agreed to drive a young lady home from school and her house was just outside my 20-minute range. She was very cute, however and her charms overruled my good sense. We would have been fine if the plows had cleared the snow from her street but as I made the turn onto her road, I got stuck in the snow. Trying to rock the car back and forth to free it, really took a toll on my already too hot motor and, with a big bang, it expired, right then...in the snow drift.

I think it cost me $35 to tow the car to the wrecking yard where I sold it for $25. Regrettably, I walked to school for the remainder of the year.

Rick Rae is publisher of the Daily Post and Citizen newspapers

CHAPTER THREE

DUEL ON THE ROAD

THE MAYFAIR BITES THE DUST

As I reminisced about my cars I penned this piece about my Beautiful little Dodge Mayfair.

The summer of 1958 was shaping up well. I was 18 and had begun work at International Harvester in Hamilton, Canada (my hometown). My father, who had been very ill with polio for many years, seemed to be improving, although he was not yet able to work full time. Between my paycheck and my Mothers, we were making ends meet.

As a result, I went car shopping and drove off the lot in a new (to me), 1954 Dodge Mayfair hardtop.

Now the Mayfair name may not be familiar to folks in the USA. In Canada, it was customary for manufacturers to brand their offerings for the Canadian market with different names. For example, the Pontiac lines had names like Pathfinder and Parisienne, and Dodges came as Mayfairs or Regents. The Royal line was offered in both countries, but in the U.S.A., the other two Dodge lines were called Coronet and Meadowbrook.

My Mayfair featured the in-line six-cylinder engine, which was the same basic engine, that was offered the year before in the Chrysler line. At 241 cubic inches it was small, but it put out 140 horsepower.

Unfortunately, the transmission in my Dodge wasn't up to the task of getting that power to the rear wheels. Dodge had come up with a semi-automatic transmission featuring a fluid coupling that they marketed as Gyro-torque drive. In Canada they called it Hy-drive. Even though you had a regular clutch, the fluid coupling allowed you to come to an idle and then drive away in high gear without shifting. That was impressive on a date, but when a '55 Olds pulled alongside at a light, it left me looking at taillights pretty quick. You could shift it manually but the fluid coupling hampered quick shifts making the torque created by the engine next to useless at stoplight getaways.

As the summer wore on, I began to make some changes to the car. The big rage back then was to have a car 'nosed' and 'decked'. That meant removing the chrome trim, filling in all the holes and running a small peak or bullnose down the center. This was before the days of fiberglass kits, so a lead bar, small torch and a body rasp were the needed tools to 'lead in' all the holes. I got a bit carried away and stripped all the chrome from the sides and top of the rear fenders as well.

After weeks of wet sanding, it was ready for the paint shop. I decided that this car deserved professional attention, so several coats of Bermuda Blue were sprayed on my treasure, hand rubbed after each coat and the application of new wide whitewalls and moon discs set it off.

My job at International Harvester's engineering department had me writing manuals and brochures on their diesel trucks. I frequently talked to my counterparts at the IHC plant in Fort Wayne, Indiana and I received an invitation from one of them for me and my family to visit and attend the upcoming Indiana State Fair.

With my father's health improving somewhat, we all packed into my Dodge for the trip to Fort Wayne.

We visited with my friend from the Harvester plant and attended the state fair with her family. When I found out that her son had an extra ticket to that weekend's Kingston Trio concert at Purdue University, it made the trip complete.

On board my Dodge, on the way back from Purdue with my friend's son and two of his buddies, a guy in a '56 Plymouth decided to test my mettle. As we sped along the two-lane blacktop in the Indiana countryside, one part of me said, *"This is stupid,"* while, another said, *"You can take that Fury!"* With the pedal floored and the needle pegged for some time, I was able to keep up but gradually the Fury moved ahead. His engine was two-years newer than mine and a bit larger.

As I pulled into Fort Wayne in the early morning hours, I noticed a good deal of smoke coming out my exhaust. The following morning as I loaded up my mom and dad for the trip back to Canada, the engine sounded really rough. As we drove homeward, the smoking increased and the power diminished. By the time we stopped for gas, it took four quarts of oil just to see a line on the dipstick. Something was seriously wrong under the hood! I nursed it homeward as the top speed dropped from 50 to 40 to 30 mph and I slowly pulled into our driveway.

The following morning, a mechanic confirmed that my engine was fried. Two of the pistons had melted, burning up the head gasket, and the back two cylinders were full of coolant. The coolant had made its way to the bearings and they were shot along with most of the other components inside.

So once again I was left on foot.

Rick Rae is president of Post Citizen Media.

CHAPTER FOUR

WIDE TRACKIN'... ALMOST

Traveling to the United States was no big deal with us but this column tells of the time that we borrowed my mother's car to vacation in Tennessee and the Carolinas.

by Rick Rae

Several months back, I began writing some columns about automobiles that I have owned. Those brought quite a bit of response from readers who asked when the next installment was coming. Others made mention of the fact that some of the cars I wrote about must have been peculiar to Canada, where I grew up, as they had never heard of them in this neck of the woods.

Some of the cars I've owned owe their lineage to The United Kingdom where cars were that were exported to Canada were more common than those sold in the USA. Others were peculiar to Canada and were not familiar to those who lived in the United States.

That set me thinking about my 1947 Monarch. In Canada, the Ford Motor Company marketed a Canadian version of the Ford, called the Meteor, as well as a Canadian version of the Mercury, called a Monarch. In 1978, they decided to market the Monarch in the U.S., but my Monarch pre-dated that one by 31 years. It looked exactly like a Mercury of the same year, but the trim was different and instead of the figure of Mercury with winged feet on the hood, it featured the likeness of a lion.

Usually, the Canadian models carried the body style similar to the American models, but the mechanicals were different. Sometimes the engines and running gear in the Canadian cars were a couple of years behind their American counterparts.

With General Motors cars, the makes were the same, but the model lines were often different. In 1963, my mother came into possession of a brand-new Pontiac Strato-Chief. In Canada, the Pontiac line began with the Pathfinder at the bottom, then to the Strato-Chief, then the Laurentian and on up to the Parisienne, which was the top of the line. There were no Gran Prix or Bonnevilles in Canadian Pontiacs, and the basic power came from a six-cylinder engine shared with Chevrolets. In fact, there was little difference between Pontiacs and Chevys.... they shared almost all the same components except the body.

Shortly after Mom got the car, Penny and I borrowed it to vacation to Florida. I'd always felt that the wheels on that Pontiac seemed too far inside the wheel wells. Somehow the body just seemed too big for the rest of the car. It wasn't until we pulled into a gas station somewhere in the Carolinas that I got a hint of what was wrong.

As we pulled up to the pumps, a fella came out of the station and started a conversation about the car. *"How do you like wide-trackin',* "he inquired.

When I asked him what he was talking about, he told me about all the new television commercials promoting the track on the all-new '63 Pontiacs. When I told him we hadn't heard about that up in Canada, he began prowling around the car looking it over.

"Well dern," he exclaimed, *"them wheels is a good foot too fer inside where they oughter be."*

Then, he popped the hood and took a look at that lonely little stovebolt six-cylinder sitting inside the huge engine compartment. *"Goshamighty,"* he wheezed as he wiped his brow with an oily rag.

"Some fool's done put a Chevy underneath this here Pontiac by mistake."

APR · 64

The photo shows Penny with the Pontiac showing off the stickers at all the campgrounds we stayed at on this trip. Notice how far the wheels are inside the fenders.

Rick Rae is president of Post-Citizen Media Inc.

CHAPTER FIVE

THE FIRST BRAND NEW CAR

I finally had saved enough money for a down payment on my first new car. Here is a column on the unusual car I ended up with.

by Rick Rae

In previous columns I discussed some adventures with my automobiles and some engine failures that were the result of them having too many miles on them, coupled with some excessive abuse on my part.

As the spring of '59 approached, I began to search for my first new set of wheels. I had saved a bit of money to cover a down payment but new cars were pretty expensive. I tested out the cars from the domestic manufacturers and one day as I was checking out the new AMC offerings, I saw a neat little job made by the British Motor Corporation called the Austin A-40.

It had some racy looks, and a peppy four-cylinder engine that would be good on gas, but most of all, it had a price tag just under $2,000. So, for a few dollars down and payments of $75 a month, I drove off the lot in my first brand new car.

This was a plain model, so I quickly made a trip to the junkyard to acquire a radio that would fit, and then to an auto parts store for a set of Port-a-Walls. Whitewall tires were a big deal in the '50s, and if you didn't have them on your car, you could buy these white rubber rings called Port-a-Walls that fit under the bead of the wheel rim. Once the tire was inflated it held the ring in place, and for $9.95 your car now sported Whitewall tires.

I lived in a little town called Ancaster, just outside Hamilton, Ontario, a Canadian city about 80 miles north of Niagara Falls. My route to work each day took me down a long winding hill, wooded on both sides. One day, while racing down this hill, a deer darted out of the woods into my path and froze. I steered left and the deer jumped right, resulting in one dead deer and one seriously damaged Austin A-40.

The car was towed to a nearby garage where I met with the-insurance adjuster and agreed to the cost of the repairs. After he left, the garage owner suggested we take the insurance settlement money and do something a little different to the Austin. The A-40 was neatly styled for the British Motor Company by Italian designer Pinin Farina. It was really a two-door station Wagon with fold-down rear seats and a drop-down tailgate in the rear. It was powered by a 948 cc in-line, 4-cylinder engine, running through a four speed, floor mounted transmission.

After a few Weeks the Austin emerged from the garage substantially altered from where it began. All the chrome trim was removed, the nose and deck were shaved and 36 louvers punched in four lines ran down both sides of the hood. This was topped by multiple coats of hand rubbed black acrylic paint. Under the hood, the engine had been bored out to 1098 cc with hand-made headers, dual straight through exhausts and cam, valve gear and twin carb intake manifold pirated from an Austin-Healey Sprite.

It was quite a bit quicker than before and boy, was it loud! The hood louvers looked pretty classy and were styled after the Cadillac-Allard sports cars and Jaguar XK-e's of that era, which sported similar louvers. Unfortunately, when it rained water came in on the distributor, which was located right on top of the engine. I solved that problem by enclosing the distributor in a rubber glove, running the four plug wires out of the fingers and the coil wire out of the thumb. Despite that, the car never ran well when it rained.

So, while all my friends were driving around in V-8 Chevies, Plymouth Furies, and other hot American cars of the late '50s and early '60s, I was driving something completely different. The Austin was still running well when I got the urge to have my first real sports car... but that's a story for another column.

Here we are camping on the Lake Erie shoreline in 1959.

Rick Rae is president of Post-Citizen Media Inc.

CHAPTER SIX

MY FIRST REAL SPORTS CAR

THE AUSTIN HEALEY SPRITE

by Rick Rae

All through the spring of 1961, I continued to drive my little Austin A-40, but the four rows of louvers I had stylishly punched in the hood created havoc on an already weak electrical system when the rains of April and May arrived. English cars all ran with Lucas electrical systems, which performed best in dry climates. Despite my best attempts to waterproof the plug wires and distributor cap, the car constantly stopped running-every time a heavy rain arrived. Perhaps that is why the managing director of the Lucas Electric Company in England is better known as "The Prince of Darkness."

On my way home one day in May, I happened to drive by Szabo Motors, the British Motor Corporation dealership, and there in the showroom, stood a pristine white, Austin-Healey Sprite. The Sprite had basically the same running gear as my Austin, but the engine was tuned a lot tighter and the body was a very sporty, two-seater sports car. An hour later, I signed off on a new loan agreement, traded the A-40, and drove off the lot in my brand-new Sprite.

The Sprite was a joy to drive, and even though the 948 cc engine generated only 60 horsepower, the car was so light it offered pretty good performance. Best of all, it was a convertible, and as the Canadian days warmed up, the top was rarely raised. Putting up the top was difficult anyway, as it had to be erected manually and the side screens had to be screwed in place on the doors. These held sliding plastic windows that were easily scratched. The top kept the sun off but wasn't much protection from rain or cold.

As always, I had to personalize the car a little so I had a paint shop run two black stripes down the tops of both fenders and bring them together in front to outline the grille. The Sprite was known as a "bug eye" in North America and was called a "frog eye" in Great Britain due to the headlights, that stuck up in the middle of the hood. The original design had them retractable, but that idea was killed to save costs.

Throughout the summer of '61 the little sports car took me back and forth between Hamilton, Ontario, and Owen Sound, a city located about 140 miles north on Georgian Bay. That was where Penny, the love of my life resided. As the Canadian winter approached, we knew the road north would be often impassable due to heavy snows, so Penny left home and took a job in my hometown.

Somehow, we survived the winter in that little Sprite, but the heater was about as effective as lighting a candle and we both had to bundle up well if we decided to drive anywhere. Penny always complained that her feet were freezing, and it wasn't until we were returning from some sports car races on a frozen lake in Northern Ontario that I took to the passenger seat and realized her side only was getting about 10 percent of what little heat was available.

The following June we got married and packed the Sprite as best we could for our honeymoon to Cape Cod. Storage space was at a premium as there was no trunk and little room in the cockpit. This meant installing a luggage rack on the rear deck where we tied on everything we needed for our two-week trip to the USA. The little "bug eye" served us well on that journey and everywhere we traveled on our way across Eastern Canada and through the New England states on our way to Massachusetts, folks would wave or honk at our heavily laden Sprite.

Rick Rae is the president of Post-Citizen Media

CHAPTER SEVEN

FAMILY MATTERS LEAD TO CHANGE IN TRANSPORTATION

THE PATHFINDER AND POLARA

When I last left my car stories I was running around in a racy little Austin-Healey Sprite. The Sprite was great in the summer, but in those cold Canadian winters it wasn't the ideal mode of transportation. That, coupled with the fact that We had decided to begin raising a family, caused me to look at modes of transportation with more than two seats.

My first venture into more traditional transportation saw me tearfully trading away the little bug-eyed Sprite for a four-year old Pontiac sedan. Now, in Canada, there were no Chieftains, Bonnevilles or Catalinas. The Canadian Pontiac line was essentially a re-badged slate of Chevrolets offered as Pathfinders, Strato-Chiefs, Laurentians and Parisiennes. I drove off the lot that day in a 1958 Pathfinder that was all black and sported a six-cylinder Chevrolet engine.

Unlike later model cars, with electric wipers, the windshield wipers on my Pontiac operated with a vacuum line running off the intake manifold. This made it difficult to see in a driving rainstorm when going up a hill. As the throttle opening increased, the vacuum decreased resulting in no wipers until you backed off the throttle. I was a little bit frustrating to drive in the rain.

It served us very well in the early sixties and was ideal for the appropriate things one takes on travels with a new baby. We traveled quite a bit to visit my wife's parents who had a cottage on Lake Huron at a place called Sauble Beach. One day, it occurred to me that it would be a great idea to load the trunk with the extremely fine white sand that was a feature of the beach and bring it home to make a sandbox for Chris, our first child.

So, I put a sheet on the floor of the trunk and began shoveling sand into the car. I filled up the whole area and was very proud of myself... until, with a creak and a groan, the entire floor of the trunk gave way and deposited the contents on the road. In Canada, as in most northern climates, it was common to use salt on the roads in the winter to help melt the ice and snow. Over time, the salt worked its' way into the crevices under the car and attacked the floor. The metal in my Pontiac had been attacked too often, and the result was that the floor began to rust away from the frame. Duct tape saved the day until we got home, but it was clear that the old Pathfinder's days were soon to be over.

Luckily, my mother's boss was in the market for a new car and made me an extremely good deal on his 1960 Dodge Polara. It had very low mileage and it sported the 383 cubic inch killer engine of that era. Although it got only nine miles per gallon, it was an exciting car to drive and turned a lot of heads with its' spaceship styling and gaudy interior. Of course, a gallon of gas cost less than 50¢ back then and that was for the larger, imperial (Canadian) gallon.

In the early sixties, Dodges had a reputation as very quick cars and despite the weight of the Polara it could easily outrun many of the called hot cars of the era and it still was a family sedan. We logged many thousands of miles on that Dodge and it served us well until I got the itch to have yet another brand-new car.

Rick Rae is president of Post-Citizen Media Inc.

CHAPTER EIGHT

SEARCH FOR THE PERFECT FAMILY CAR

THE ANGLIA AND CORTINA

by Rick Rae

As our family grew in the mid- 60s, with the addition of Chris in '64 and Kit in '66, the cost of putting gasoline into our 1960 Dodge Polara with the high-output 383-cubic-inch engine got to be a significant factor. Even at cheap 1960s prices, 9 mpg isn't the kind of mileage you want when trying to raise a couple of kids.

So, we began to look at more economical modes of transportation. Ford was making inroads into the Canadian market at that time, and its offerings exported from England featured economical engines with room for four. Another car I liked was the Chevy Corvair, but Ralph Nader had just written his book "Unsafe at any Speed," and we were just a bit leery of that product as a result.

One day, we visited the Ford dealership and took a '66 Anglia 105E out for a test drive. This little wonder marked a complete break with tradition in the light car field and had quickly established itself as a best-seller on the world market. In many ways, the Anglia design was ahead of its time. The distinctive rear-sloping back window and frog-like eyes made it very different from any other small vehicle on the road at the time. Ford also went in for colors that no one had even dared consider. Ford Anglias were built in primrose yellow, light green and even with two tones.

We drove a DeLuxe model with full-width plated grille, bright metal windshield trim, chrome side strips and chrome light bezels. The interior appointments were outstanding and featured leather seats and trim. Under the hood was a completely new overhead valve engine. This lightweight, high-revving 4-cylinder 997cc ohv engine developed 59 bhp at 5000 rpm and had a 4-speed gearbox.

After negotiating a suitable trade price for the Dodge, we drove off in our new mist green car with a contrasting dark green interior and traded 9 mpg for about 26 mpg, which allowed us to buy a lot of diapers for Kit the newest addition to the family.

That car took us on our first vacation deep into the United States, all the way to Key West, Fla. We left the deep, February snowdrifts of Ontario and reveled in the Florida sunshine. We had hitched a travel trailer to the back of the little Ford, and the car pulled it with some effort on that vacation and a few others. A fully loaded Anglia, plus trailer, however, wasn't the best thing in the world for an engine of less than a liter, and so the following year we opted for something a little bigger. That, plus the fact that Brett, our third child, was due any day took us back for another look at what Ford had to offer.

The next model up from the Ford Anglia was the Cortina. The Cortina had been launched in Mark I version a few years earlier and, in collaboration with Colin Chapman of the Lotus Company, offered a Lotus Cortina using the Lotus 1250 cc engine, twin Weber carburetors, disc brakes and a racing suspension. The factory version of this was called the Cortina GT, and the model I fell for was the Mark II estate wagon version of the GT.

By '67, the engine used in the GT was a five main bearing, 1498 cc high-revving engine that just tickled 100 horsepower. This engine, coupled with a close ratio, four speed gearbox, provided a lot of oomph, but the car still had room for Mom, Dad, three kids and the usual stuff that accompanies them on trips.

It seemed like the ideal car for us, but I had a bad habit of exceeding the 6,000 rpm redline on that engine and ended up "floating" the valves quite a bit. Oil consumption got to be a major problem with this car as the valve seals grew weak and, despite repeated trips back to the dealer, we were never able to control oil consumption down to much less than a quart every 500 miles or so. After fighting with the dealer for many months, I finally made the decision to trade it away on something a bit stronger.

I still liked Fords, but now I was thinking about Galaxies that put out over 300 horsepower from engines that displaced 390 cubic inches. But that is a column for another time.

Rick Rae is publisher if the Daily Post.

CHAPTER NINE

LARGER ENGINES NEEDED

A GALAXIE XL AND HILLMAN MINX

My last column had me ready to give up on foreign built cars with small engines and move to something a little more substantial. By now, we had two kids in the family with one on the way, so spending money on a new car was out of the question. I shopped the lots and finally decided to trade in to a 1966 Ford Galaxie 500, two door hardtop.

Although I wanted one with the 390 or 406 cubic inch engine, I had to settle for the 352 FE. It was still a pretty good motor with the factory four barrel and I think it put out around 280 horsepower and that was a good bit of giddyup in 1968.

My neighbor in Toronto was a high school auto mechanic teacher and so my Galaxie became a project car for his class. Off came the stock exhaust manifolds to be replaced by a set of headers, dumping into a pair of Thrush glass-pack mufflers. We didn't have any catalytic converters to worry about in those days. They also sent out the heads to be machined to bump up the compression ratio and then worked on the intake manifold and heads to polish up the innards to improve the flow and add more horsepower.

The dual glass-packs on that Ford emitted the best sound of any car I have even owned. I put a new set of Uniroyal Tiger Paws on the car and then did my best to make slicks out of the pair on the back. One of my co-workers announced my entrance to the company parking area... *"Here comes the cool cat with his Hollywood mufflers..* Another called my new tires *"Tiger Pause".*

Not long after getting the car the way I wanted it I was transferred from Toronto to Winnipeg that was about 2,500 miles to the northwest and a whole lot colder. In Toronto I was able to take the subway back and forth to work but I needed the car all day in Winnipeg, so we started to shop for something inexpensive for Penny.

I was always a sucker for something unusual and stumbled on a 1951 Hillman Minx Californian, two-door hardtop. It had a lot of scars on the body but sounded okay mechanically. Since it was almost impossible to find parts for this rare British-built car I picked it up cheaply. Once Penny placed a lot of flower decals over the rust spots we had a neat little car. Because of her decor the kids called it "The Flowerpot".

This little car had an interesting time in the very, very cold Winnipeg winter which usually lasted from Labor Day through May Day each year. At temperatures around 10-15 below zero it was impossible to shift the transmission. Even with the lightest gear oil I could find, it would just get so syrupy that you couldn't shift from first to second gear until it had been running for ten minutes or more. Also, the nylon tires went flat on the bottom in the cold and went "thump, thump, thump" for the first five or six miles until they became round again. The Galaxie seemed to handle the weather much better.

That summer we decided to travel into the Rockies and so I had a hitch put on the Galaxie and we rented a travel trailer. With four kids in tow, we packed up and headed west, across the plains, through Saskatchewan and Alberta to visit Banff and Jasper National parks. The modified engine in the Ford handled the mountain roads well despite the weight of the trailer, but coming home across the wilds of northern Saskatchewan was another story.

It was late in the afternoon and we were running along an unpaved road in Northern Saskatchewan at a pretty good clip, looking for a campground, when I hit the mother of all potholes. The car bottomed out and a rock knocked a huge hole in the pipe leading from the manifold to the muffler on one side. With the car sounding like a tank and fumes coming in under the floorboards, there was no garage in sight. In fact, there wasn't even a town for miles.

Ever resourceful, I found an empty oil can at the side of the road and flattened it out with my heel. (*Those were the days before plastic oil containers*). I then got a wire coat-hanger out of the trunk and twisted the wire over the pipe to secure the flattened oil can in place. It still leaked a bit but the noise was abated and with the windows rolled down we limped on in search of the campground. The next day, I added a piece of tin I found to my home-made patch and secured it with more coat hanger wire. That patch stayed on for the next 400 miles back home. It wasn't until I got home that I discovered my bout with the hole in the road had also damaged the front suspension and oil pan. As I weighed the cost of repairs against the cost of another car, the decision to move on to another vehicle wasn't hard to make.

That led us on to The Ukranian Easter Egg!

CHAPTER TEN

ROAD TRIP TO THE USA

THE UKRAINIAN EASTER EGG

When last I left our readers we were living in Winnipeg, Manitoba, where they describe the climate as "nine months of winter and three months of poor sledding."

Our '66 Galaxie had just bit the dust, and I got my first taste of what it means to be financially "upside down" on a car. In a nutshell, we owed more on the old Galaxie than it was worth. Compounding the problem was the fact that I had accepted the company transfer from Toronto to Winnipeg without analyzing what the difference in cost of living was between the two cities. While it was described as a promotion, the small amount of salary increase didn't come close to offsetting the higher living costs in western Canada.

On top of that we had decided to adopt a baby girl. We had tried to have a family of one boy and one girl, but after three tries we ended up with three boys. We just knew we would have a fourth boy the routine way, so we decided to adopt, if possible. Not only was it possible, but we ended up bringing Lana home with us less than a month after we applied. We had expected a wait of six to eight months, so we now had four kids and two of them still in diapers.

As a result, our automobile needs became secondary, and I downgraded to a '64 Chevrolet station wagon that had quite a few miles on it. The previous owner apparently had not liked the blue exterior color with the white top, so it had been repainted. The middle portion of the car was purple, the lower part was black, and the white top and blue interior remained. Winnipeg has a large Ukrainian population, and they liked to wear very bright colors. As a result, one of my coworkers, who was of Ukrainian descent, called my Chevy, "the Ukrainian Easter Egg."

I had worked hard all through 1971 and declined to take a vacation. Penny wasn't enthralled about living in Winnipeg where winters start on Labor Day, the temperature goes down to 10 below zero and stays there until spring arrives sometime in May.

As I came home one day in April of 1972, there was the purple station wagon in the driveway with a Stuery travel trailer hitched to the back. I rushed in the house to find out what was going on and was met with Penny's response. *"We are leaving on vacation in the morning, we're worn out with this winter. You're welcome to come with us."*

I quickly called my boss, explained the situation and decided to take a two-week vacation starting the next day. As with all our trips, we kept a daily diary. I checked out the diary for this column and noted that we left for Bismarck, N.D., at 7:30 a.m. on Friday, April 28, 1972. What a trip it was.

In all we traveled 7,129 miles and took longer than two weeks. We visited Mount Rushmore in South Dakota. The Black Hills, Colorado Springs; Pike's Peak; Santa Fe, New Mexico; The Petrified Forest; The Grand Canyon and Phoenix. So taken were we with the American Southwest that I called my boss and arranged for third week of absence and then wired the bank for more money. With a bit more cash and a new set of tires we moved on to Lake Mead, Nevada; the Hoover Dam; Las Vegas; Death Valley, California and kept heading west to Yosemite.

The 283 V-8 in the Chevy kept churning along, but as we got to Death Valley at 400 feet below sea level, the radiator overheated and blew. I nursed it to a service center in Panamint Springs and discovered the water pump was cracked. When I asked the cost to install a new one the response was $50. When I told the guy I would install it myself I was quoted the same $50 without installation, *"take it or leave it!"* So, we filled every container that would hold water and began the long climb out of the valley to Yosemite, stopping frequently to cool things off and replace water that steamed out of the radiator. Finally, I babied the car to Oakland, California where I visited an auto parts store and bought a water pump for $12.95. I installed it that evening while Penny made dinner over the Coleman stove in the campground.

We then moved on to San Francisco and up the coast to the Redwood Forest and into Oregon. Money was getting tight by now, so we wired back and made the bank account dangerously low. I called my boss and negotiated more time. We pulled into British Columbia, visited Vancouver and then started back home over the Rocky Mountains, through Alberta and

Saskatchewan, to Winnipeg. On May 29, we pulled into our driveway, which was still full of snow.

Our oldest boy had an extreme allergy and it wasn't until we got home that we realized he'd had no breathing problems all the time we were away. Turns out, he was allergic to a peculiar type of mold that is prevalent in Manitoba. The company sympathized with our problem and arranged a transfer to another of their properties located in a friendlier climate in southern Ontario. It wasn't long after that our travels brought us permanently to the United States.

(The accompanying photo shows the Ukrainian Easter Egg being attacked by wild burros in Death Valley.

Rick Rae is president of Post-Citizen newspapers Inc.

CHAPTER ELEVEN

Sometimes other newspapers requested my services to write a column or opinion piece for them. In this case, my old newspaper employer in Canada was preparing a series called "the Memory Project" and were looking for recollections on events from the past. This was the column of mine that they published.

JOE HYND AND THE GOLDEN CUE

SPECIAL TO THE SPECTATOR'S MEMORY SERIES BY RICK RAE

I started working at the Hamilton Spectator in 1966 It was my first venture into the newspaper business as an advertising salesperson. Back in those times there was a pool hall called the Golden Cue located upstairs, next to the Spectator building in downtown Hamilton. It was customary for those of us in the ad department to spend our lunch hour there, either to play in or watch the matches. Joe was a co-worker and we played many times and battled one another well past the lunch hour and into what was referred to as "company time."

Joe didn't talk much about his past, but rumor had it that he had been born into a wealthy Hamilton family and was destined to take over the family business. Apparently, Joe's family frowned on his gambling and pool playing and warned that if it continued, he would not be welcome in the business. With that, Joe took cue in hand and traveled Canada and the United States, making a living at the pool halls he visited during the great Depression years. After his father died, Joe returned to Hamilton and although he inherited enough to make him comfortable, he was indeed, never welcomed into the family business.

One day, as we left the pool hall, Joe commented, *"you shoot a pretty good stick. How would you like to make some real money with it later this week?"* He said he had a snooker game lined up for that Friday at the Royal Hamilton Yacht Club. I later learned he had been a member of the club for some time and had a large vintage Chris Craft maintained there.

Friday, I arrived at the appointed time and after showing me around, Joe introduced me to two local businessmen who would be our opponents for a team match of snooker. Joe took me aside and whispered that although we were playing for fairly large stakes, I was not to worry about money as he *"had me covered. Just play your usual game,"* he advised. *"Don't get nervous and don't have more than a couple of drinks"*.

The Yacht Club tables were gorgeous, heavy slate, six by twelve-foot wonders with deep, woven leather pockets. Those old oak tables rolled as true as any I had ever seen. I think we began playing around 7 p.m. and were still racking them up well into the next morning. As we pulled on our coats and headed up the driveway, Joe handed me a wad of money, representing my share of the evening's proceeds.

It wasn't until later in the morning that I rolled open the money to discover that I had made more money the night before than I had in the previous two weeks selling ad space for the Spectator.

Over the course of the next couple of years at the Spec, I partnered Joe in several games of snooker, Russian billiards and straight pool that supplemented our income extremely well during the early years of our marriage.

Rick Rae is a former Hamilton resident who now resides in Loganville, Georgia. He worked at The Spectator from 1966 to 1969. He is now publisher of the Rockdale Citizen, a daily newspaper published in Conyers, Georgia.

CHAPTER TWELVE

The Spectator came calling again a few years later so I wrote this piece for them about some memories from the fifties.

CONWAY TWITTY STOLE MY GIRL

IT'S ONLY MAKE BELIEVE COMES TO LIFE

Special to the Hamilton Spectator By Rick Rae

I caught a piece of a song from the' 50s channel on XM radio the other night that brought back a flood of memories. The song was "It's Only Make Believe" from 1959. You trivia buffs out there know that this song was first recorded by Conway Twitty, but this story goes much deeper than that.

In the fall of 1958, I was living in my hometown of Hamilton, Ontario. Hamilton is just over the Canadian border about 60 miles north of Buffalo. I was dating a girl named Carole and on Thursday and Friday evenings we would drop into the Flamingo lounge to listen to the rock 'n' roll acts that appeared there. One of our favorites was a guy from Arkansas named Harold Jenkins, who played some guitar and had a growly voice that handled the late' 50s hits he covered pretty well. Between sets he would sit at our table, probably attracted more by Carole's blond good looks than by my stirring conversation.

Hal was just one of many singers from the United States who found their way to Canada in the 50's. Promoters like Harold Kudlets would book them into a circuit of Southern Ontario towns, probably figuring if they could make it in those towns, they could have potential to go to the big time back home.

Interestingly enough, three Arkansas boys hit the Southern Ontario circuit about the same time. Ronnie Hawkins played the Cote d'Or in Toronto backed by a drummer named Levon Helm, and then there was Hal Jenkins. His curly hair and good looks were set off well in the beautiful turquoise '56 Oldsmobile convertible he drove.

In the spring of 1959, Jenkins returned to Canada for another booking, but things had changed a lot. He had just cut a record titled "It's Only Make Believe" and it was climbing the charts. He also had a new name. We still called him Hal, but the poster out front of the lounge said he was Conway Twitty.

"The promoters told me, he said, "that Harold Jenkins wasn't a strong enough name for a performer. So, I took the road Atlas and plunked my thumb and forefinger down on two towns. One was Conway, Arkansas, and the other was Twitty, Texas."

Now whether that was the truth on how his name came to be, didn't matter... Carole just sat there mesmerized by the story and the song.

On the way home that night things were a little tense between us as I complained about the attention she showered on good ol' Hal between sets. Her response made things even colder when she suggested that maybe I ought to stay home Saturday so we could spend some time away from each other. Now that was a long time ago, but I think I burned some rubber as I let her off, popped the clutch on the old flathead and tore away from her home.

A bit of remorse set in on Saturday morning and I decided to swallow my pride and drive over to Carole's house to make up. As I drove down her street, I couldn't help but notice the turquoise ' 56 Oldsmobile convertible with Arkansas plates in her driveway. Good ol' Hal was bird-doggin' my girl. The irony of it all was that as I drove away in disgust, "It's Only Make. Believe" came on the radio in my car.

Rick Rae is a former Hamilton resident who now resides in Loganville, Georgia. He worked at The Spectator from 1966 to 1969. He is now publisher of the Rockdale Citizen, a daily newspaper published in Conyers, Georgia.

CHAPTER THIRTEEN

GREAT LAKES MOTORCYCLE TRIP

The urge to write columns in the newspaper began well before I became a publisher. When we first came to the United States I was recruited to be the advertising manager of the Oakland Press located in Pontiac Michigan.

In 1974 we began an adventure that took us back to Canada on a trip around Lake Superior on our motorcycles. I bugged the editor to let me write about it in the newspaper and after I submitted a very long piece he gave me to the space to publish it. We got a lot of positive feedback from this column.

LAKE SUPERIOR TRIP JULY 1974

The crack and roar of one, then another twin cylinder engine shatters the silence of the damp predawn July air. Visors snap down and zippers snug into place. Heavy boots kick through the gears as the machines roll out onto the asphalt.

The sound of four exhaust pipes echoes off the shuttered windows and locked doors. At 5 AM this Drayton Plains, Michigan subdivision is a very quiet place. In tight formation the bikes turn north on M 15 and lazily lean into the turns as the sun reflects through the trees on highly polished chrome.

The motorcycles are Hondas.

In the vernacular of the enthusiast they are fully dressed. Windshield fairings, saddlebags, Luggage racks, sissy bars and CB radios are some of the items that indicate these bikes are tourers, ready for the highway.

Early morning shadows flee the sunshine that reveals more about these motorized intruders. One of the bikes is bright pink with millions of metalflake sparkles winking through. Astride the machine is a form in tightfitting leathers topped with a pink helmet that matches the color scheme of the motorcycle.

No masculine machine this! Its gender is obvious, which, by design affords its rider more courtesy than shown other riders. The helmet turns, revealing an attractive face, even white teeth and an unruly lock of blond hair bobbing against the face shield.

By contrast, the companion machine is drab even though its' metallic avocado finish stands out among stock machines.

The bikes are small by touring standards, displacing a mere 360 ccs. Most tourers are 500s, 750s or even 1000s. Despite their engine size these motorcycles are capable of cruising at 55 mph. 70 or even 80 is there if needed.

In the two months preceding this day the riders have covered more than 3000 miles on these very machines. That 3000 happens to be their total motorcycle experience as they purchased and learned to ride the bikes just this year.

The lady is Penny....Artist, roller skater, tailor, sailor, mother of four and now a biker. She's also my wife.

Our adventure started on impulse when we decided that motorcycling may be fun. The salesman was apprehensive when we asked for lessons but as that was the condition of his sale, he reluctantly agreed. Now, two months later we were on our way.

We headed towards the Canadian border crossing at Port Huron, Ontario. North from Sarnia we traveled the Lake Huron shoreline under cloudless cobalt skies. Goderich, Southampton, Kincardine and Port Elgin are a few of the picturesque towns along the Huron shoreline. Our destination this day is Sauble Beach, sometimes called the Daytona of Canada. Originally one could drive the entire 12 miles of hard packed sand along the beach but now less than 4 miles is open to traffic.

After seeing the sun safely to rest over the beach we found a quiet cabin for the night. Our initial plan was to take the ferry from the town of Tobermory across Georgian Bay to the island of Manitoulin and then travel to the north shore of Lake Superior. But to our surprise the ferry was over-booked and the waiting period was expected to be between five and seven hours. A quick conference over breakfast led us to the decision to go around rather than across Georgian Bay.

Dark, forbidding clouds greeted us as we roared onto the highway. Cautiously we made our way along the southern shoreline. Owen Sound, Craigleith, and Collingwood. Towns that were established by the Ojibway Indians and early Scottish settlers. Collingwood is world renowned for its blue Mountain pottery as well as its' ski slopes.

We turned northward along the Georgian Bay coast and the names of the places became more exotic.... Wabaushene, Penetanguishene, and Wasaga carry their Indian heritage proud. Then comes Parry sound, Home of a fairly competent hockey player by the name of Bobby Orr.

We had hoped to reach Sudbury by nightfall but the excellent trans-Canada four-lane made travel easy and we arrived in the mining country by midafternoon. This part of Canada is the northern crust of the Precambrian, or Canadian Shield. Scrub trees, little vegetation and beautiful lava-like glacial rock mark the rugged landscape. Sudbury, Copper Cliff, Falconbridge and

Creighton Mine all sit on top of the copper, silver uranium and other precious minerals located and mined here.

We pushed along trans-Canada Highway 17 through Espanola to Webwood where we located a comfortable motel. Throughout our trip we approached motels somewhat apprehensively never knowing how they would react to motorcyclists. We never had a problem.

Next morning was a cool mid 40 overcast day. We kick the bikes to life and headed westward along the north channel. It has taken us all day to get to the point where the ferry would have dropped us after a two-hour ferry ride. Shortly after lunch we pass through Sault Ste. Marie and began heading north along the shore of Lake Superior. This is rough country. Superior is the largest of the Great Lakes and is held in awe by those who sail it.

Highway 17 begins climbing and twisting at this point and we let our bikes lean through the long sweeping turns. Late afternoon finds us cresting Ogidaki mountain, Ontario's highest point, then we begin the downhill run to Wawa. This is motorcycling at its most enjoyable state. Machine and rider become almost one as we swoop down through the switchbacks and S -turns and too quickly the town of Wawa looms up ahead.

The Wawa hotel is an excellent resort that features fine food and an Olympic size pool. The sauna boasts a panoramic view of Gitchi-Gumi, the Ojibway name for Lake Superior. Over dinner Penny relives the afternoon ride. The hairpin turn after we left Goulais River that shoots the highway out over Batchawana bay. The quiet beauty of the Montréal River area where giant maples stand guard over the rugged Shoreline. We plan the next day and hope to arrive in Thunder Bay by mid-afternoon. The single radio station sends us to bed with a warning of cold weather for the next day.

The Canadian broadcasting Company announcer was correct. 3°C is darn close to freezing. On go sweaters, then the leather jackets, then nylon jackets make up the next layer over which we pull our vinyl rain-suits. Very stiffly we waddled to our motorcycles. The cozy hotel room was much better than the cold northern highway that awaits.

The road leaves the shore, and for the next 50 miles we cut through the wild Canadian bush. The unusual odor of the pulp and paper mills begins to permeate the brisk forest air. About noon we turn westward, back toward the shore and the icy wind coming from Lake Superior hits us with full force. We shiver into White River which holds the distinction of being the coldest spot ever recorded in Canada. A temperature of 72°

below zero was recorded here in the early 50s. it doesn't feel much warmer than that today.

Lunch is accompanied by several cups of hot chocolate and afterward we gas up our bikes. Another Honda roars up to the pumps and the rider slowly eases off his machine. Four layers of clothing topped by a Royal Canadian Air Force all weather suit have kept him reasonably warm since yesterday noon. He has cycled across the Canadian Prairie from Moose Jaw, Saskatchewan, stopping only for fuel and is now 26 hours on the road, heading for Montreal, Quebec. We wish the lone rider well and go in our separate directions.

The odor of the pulp mills of Marathon, Terrace Bay and Schreiber soon assail our nostrils. The damp dark clouds hold the fumes close to the ground. Rain spots appear on our windshields and we begin looking for cover.

Two wheels are more maneuverable than four on dry pavement but not when it's slick. Very early in our cycling careers we gained great respect for wet roads. As the rain intensifies, we cut speed and finally pull over to the shoulder on a hill overlooking Nipigon Bay. The downpour turns into a raging torrent as water cascades down the embankment and out over the roadway.

We quickly park our machines and rush for cover under some nearby trees. A station wagon honks as we cut across the median and pulls to a stop.

"Hey", shouts the driver. *"We'll make room in the back and you can stay in the car until it lets up."*

We thank the couple but explain that we are already so wet that it wouldn't help very much. Once settled under a tree we sit back in clammy discomfort and survey our bikes framed by an angry sky and a whitecapped Lake.

Suddenly the machine closest to the lake begins to move. The torrent of water running over the road has eroded the soft shoulder. The motorcycle was standing on that shoulder. We jump to our feet and watch helplessly as the bike shifts and crashes towards the lake.

"My motorcycle," cries Penny! "It's gone". We slosh across the roadway fearing the worst. Penny's bike is nowhere to be seen...

We climb the shoulder and there, leaning over the guard rail is the pink Honda. Just two strands of cable linking the posts are all that is keeping her motorcycle from plunging down into Lake Superior. After much straining and grunting we manage to get the 600 pound machine upright. It is still raining but at this point we couldn't be any wetter, so we mount and move slowly onward.

Our fear of rain slicked pavement keeps our speed well under 40 miles an hour. Then a road sign informs us that thunder Bay is less than 100 miles away. At the rate we're going we may make it by dark.

As the shadows lengthen, the cold dampness settles into our weary bodies. our friends in Thunder Bay are expecting us at any time. The thought crosses my mind that a phone call could bring a warm car out to meet us on the highway. Another part of my mind says that would be the coward's way. We have been colder and damper than this. My mind then becomes occupied with trying to recall when that was. While all these mental gymnastics are going on miles have been covered and we finally arrive at our destination. A couple of a potent rum drinks later, the cold and the dampness are just vivid memories.

Our plans are to remain in Thunder Bay for a few days and then head south around the extreme west end of the lake to Duluth Minnesota. From Duluth we will cross over into Wisconsin, back through upper Michigan and then homeward.

Somewhere along the way the tachometer on my Honda has stopped telling me how fast the engine is turning. The next morning I'm up early and off to the local Honda dealer. The bearded proprietor doesn't have the part I need in stock but while he's checking the bike he tells me it's not running as smoothly as it should. Two hours later the Honda is purring like I've never heard and my Canadian mechanic friend refuses to accept payment. "You came here for a tach", he explains, "the tune-up is my way of apologizing for not having it in stock."

Over the next couple of days, we tour the Thunder Bay area. The city of Thunder Bay was formed by the merger of the twin cities of Port Arthur and Fort William. It boasts an excellent harbor and is the pulp and paper center in this part of Canada. My friend Bob and I leave the next morning for a trip up the Kaministikwia River in his Boston Whaler. We start up the river from the harbor, surrounded on both sides by towering grain elevators. Thunder Bay is also the railhead where wheat from Saskatchewan and Manitoba is stored after traveling across the prairies. We follow the river upstream to the site of the original Fort William until the roaring whitewater of the rapids forces our return. Were we able to journey further upstream we would be at the foot of Kekabeka Falls which supplies the city's hydroelectric power.

The comfortable hospitality of our friends makes it difficult to leave but we decide to head south the following day. Dawn breaks with angry dark clouds overhead. Rain is in the air but we decide to get on our way. There is little traffic on the road all the way to the border, as the lightning flashes in the distance and the roll of thunder is all around us. But the rain doesn't fall.

The border crossing consists of one building and the gate. The guard gives us a curious good morning and wishes us a safe trip to Duluth.

All morning we travel under the black clouds along the western shoreline of Lake Superior. The temperature is pleasant when trees shield us from the wind, but when it comes straight off the water we shiver from the chill.

We ride into Duluth in the midst of noon hour traffic. The sun has broken through and we experience the warmest afternoon of our trip so far. Our stay in Minnesota is brief and we start across the bridge to Superior Wisconsin. There we stop for lunch at a Holiday Inn located right on the lake. After lunch we step out of the air-conditioned Inn into what seems like a furnace. The temperature has climbed to the low 80s on the southern side of the lake so we pack away the leather jackets.

The highway seems to be reserved for us alone as we cycle along the shore with a warm wind against her bare arms. It seems hours before we see any traffic and we revel in the solitude, the warmth of the lake and the Wisconsin scenery.

There's still plenty of daylight left as we check in at the Lakeside Motel and lock our bikes beside the room. A stroll along the shore before dinner leads us to a roadside park with historical markers indicating that a fort once stood here. Radisson and Grosseilliers, the French explorers landed here and erected a fort. Their expedition wintered here before continuing westward to the Lake of the Woods.

We find our most presentable clothes and dress up for dinner. An enjoyable meal relaxes us and we review the events of the day. Tomorrow holds great promise if the weather continues and we turn in for the night with our fingers crossed.

It's a great day. The sun is bright, the sky is blue the clouds are puffy and white. We fire up the motorcycles and head southeast on the two-lane towards Michigan's upper Peninsula. It's such a lazy day that we decide to stay off the main roads and do some exploring.

Near Iron River the road bridges a small stream, crossing to a little park that is nestled by the Bridge. We turn our bikes down the hill beside the water and while Penny wanders up stream I stretch out and engage in some cloud watching.

The roar of a pink motorcycle startles me awake. *"come on sleepyhead, we'll never get home at this rate"*, admonishes my partner. Keeping to the back roads we cross over into Michigan and lunch at a very forgettable restaurant/grocery store/post office/gas station. The flies that fill the place will eat better than we do this day. We quickly fuel up and get on our way.

After about a half hour on the road I notice an uncomfortable itch on top of my head. The itch seems to spread and I push my helmet back to scratch a bit. The itch spreads. Finally, my whole head seems to be on fire. I pull off the road and yank off my helmet, but that offers little relief.

Penny has noticed me missing and returns to see what the problem is. Together we assume that I may have played host to some sand or grass fleas while dozing in the long grass beside the stream we visited earlier. Whatever the cause it's damned uncomfortable. The absurd idiocy of helmet laws is my next problem. Here we are, all alone on this road and our cruising speed is under 50 miles an hour with no traffic and yet there is a state law which says I cannot let the wind blow through my hair to soothe my tortured head. I break the law and we get underway. Our destination is Escanaba, Michigan.

Because we're behind schedule we swing back to the main highway near Crystal Falls. Reason dictates that I must now wear my helmet as traffic is picking up. About 15 minutes of this is all I can stand and I'm ready to rip it off in tear out my hair. A small town is coming up and I race into a gas station restroom, dousing my head in the sink full of cold water nearly brings me back to normal.

If there are little critters in my hair I stay under long enough to do 'em in. Rejuvenated, I'm ready to ride all night. We pass Escanaba in midafternoon and head for Manistique. Our spurt of energy was just that however, a spurt. We find a motel on the Lake, halfway to a place called Bay de Noc. The bikes get locked up, the chains get oiled and we head for the beach.

As the sun sets in the water we walk along the shoreline communicating without words. The chill of dusk awakes us to how far we have walked. The sun has set by the time we return to the motel. It's been a good day, sore head aside.

Morning brings a repeat of yesterday's weather. Today we are home if we can handle 500 miles. Traffic is light and the motorcycles seem to sense we're homeward bound. The beautiful Mackinac Bridge looms ahead. At the toll booths we spot a large group of motorcyclists heading north. We wave in the accepted motorcyclist's salute and start across the bridge.

Gaylord, Grayling, West Branch... the signs click off as we cruise down Interstate 75. We leave the interstate south of Bay City to take Highway 15 toward Drayton Plains. Oddly enough our first instance of motorcycle discrimination pops up less than 100 miles from home. We are due for a gasoline stop and I'm ready for a stop of another kind. I pull into the station and jump off the bike to get into the restroom.

This surly attendant informs me that "the can is for customers and no bikers are allowed." I didn't bother informing him that he just lost two customers. We made our stop a bit further down the road.

Home is just a few miles away and we quicken the pace anxious to see the kids. Sometimes it seems that the nicest part of a trip away from home is the feeling you get upon returning. As we roll into the driveway Penny's odometer tells us we've traveled 2694 miles since leaving nine days ago. We're happy to be home, but in the back of our minds the plan for our next trip is starting to incubate.

We are hooked.

Rick Rae is the regional Advertising Director of the Oakland Press

CHAPTER FOURTEEN

THE CAMARO Z-28 PROJECT

The year was 1981. The preceding year, I had been promoted to Gatlinburg, Tennessee to be president and publisher of the Mountain Press Publishing Company, a newly acquired division of Harte-Hanks Communications. This was my first publisher position in the company and saw me overseeing the operations of two newspapers, a shopper and two tourist publications produced by the division.

Two days after beginning my new job, a fire broke out in the cluttered attic of the printing plant and the entire facility burned to the ground. Over the next year we continued to produce our products, find a new home and re-establish ourselves in the community. At the same time, we continued to make improvements to this profitable property that the owners had purchased.

As a small reward, for my efforts the company president informed me that the company car I had been driving could be replaced by a more expensive one of my choice within the guidelines of our company policy.

I now had a budget of $12,000, which in today's money would be close to $40,000, to shop for a new car. The car I had admired through the sixties and late seventies was the Chevrolet Camaro. Launched as the answer to Ford's Mustang in 1966, the Camaro had evolved over the years to become the performance king of the muscle-car era, especially the Z-28 version.

Entering the showroom of Al Smith Chevrolet in downtown Sevierville Tennessee I spotted the car I wanted right way. A 1981 Z-28 Camaro that had just been unloaded off the transport. The car was painted in dark red that Chevrolet called Carmine and I couldn't wait to test drive it. The 5.7 liter engine didn't appear to have as much power as I expected but I continued to make the deal and traded away the 1979 AMC Concord I had been driving for the previous two years.

Although I loved the styling I was not enthralled with the performance. On the way back home, I pulled up at a red light beside a 300 ZX and he proceeded to leave me in the dust when the light turned green. I was convinced that car was low on power. The following week I took it to a performance shop in nearby Maryville to have it evaluated.

After checking it out the technician gave me a list he felt the engine required. "First off, all that emission and anti-pollution stuff has to come off so the engine can breathe properly. Then we have to open it up with a set of headers and low back pressure glasspacks so the exhaust gasses don't continue to choke the engine. Next, we have to increase the size of the fuel injectors and install a Mallory ignition system to give us a hotter spark in order to burn the additional fuel. Once we install a transmission shifter kit, that ought to be enough to bring that 5.7 liter engine to life and let it run like a genuine Z-28."

The following week, I drove it away and immediately noticed the difference when I blew off a guy in a Monte Carlo at a stoplight on the way home. Another big difference I noticed was how quickly I wore out those big Goodyear, Gatorbacks on the back end.

Over the next several months I grew to love my Z-28 but what I didn't love was the number of speeding tickets that I collected. Between the Sevier County Sheriff's department, the police departments in the cities of Sevierville, Pigeon Forge, and Gatlinburg and the Federal cops who patrolled the Smoky Mountains National Park; I think they took turns seeing who could give me the most number of tickets.

Then I received a letter from the Tennessee Department of Safety instructing me to visit the closest office of the Tennessee Highway Patrol to take a test and explain to them why I should retain my Tennessee driver's license.

As I drove up in front of the office, I met Buford Oakley, a THP sergeant I knew well. *"Rick, I know why you're here. That damn car you are driving is like waving red flag in front of a bull when viewed by one of our THP officers! You need to be driving something more sedate and less noticeable."* With that, he administered the written and driving tests that were required, filled out a lot of forms and sent me on my way.

The following week I swapped my treasured Camaro Z-28 even up with a local dealer for a pretty bronze Cadillac Fleetwood Brougham and never had another traffic citation.

Rick Rae is president of the Mountain Press

CHAPTER FIFTEEN

MY MERCURY

DISCOVERING THE HOUSE OF BLUE LIGHTS

This one brings back memories of cruising the back roads of Southern Ontario at age fifteen without a care in the world.

In the summer of 1955, I ventured down to City Chevrolet in Hamilton where for $250 I purchased my first automobile. It was a 1947 Mercury two door coupe with about 80,000 miles on it. In addition to the 'glass pack' mufflers we installed in my friend's father's Texaco station, I mounted tiny 'blue dot' spotlights inside the upper corners of the windshield. They cast a blue highlight down over the dashboard and were sold as a device to reduce the glare from oncoming headlights. They would soon be outlawed in Canada but they continued in the USA for a few years thereafter to be the thing that designated you as a 'very cool' driver'.

One of the first cruises I took in that dark blue coupe was down Longwood Road, under the High Level bridge to the Valley Inn Road. There was a little place called The Willow Cove Post Office owned by the Easterbrook family, that not only served the best foot long hot dogs but they had the most complete music selections on their juke box. I pulled in just at dusk and the speakers on the porch were blaring out a song called The House of Blue Lights. The strains of that song, coupled with the reflection of my own blue lights hitting the windshield made an indelible mark on my psyche.

The song was published in 1946, written by Don Raye and Freddie Slack. It was first recorded by Freddie Slack with singer Ella Mae Morse and was covered the same year by The Andrews Sisters. Notably for the time, the song featured a "hipster" spoken introduction by Raye and Morse.......

"Well, whatcha say, baby? You look ready as Mr. Freddy this black. How 'bout you and me goin' spinnin' at the track?" What's that, homie? If you think I'm goin' dancin' on a dime, your clock is tickin' on the wrong time." "Well, what's your pleasure, treasure? You call the plays, I'll dig the ways. "Hey daddy-o, I'm not so crude as to drop my mood on a square from way back......."

For some reason I was unaware of the earlier versions of the song and thought that I had discovered a brand new goodie that night. When I went inside to check on the artist the label told me that the recording was by Chuck Miller.

In 1955 he moved to Mercury Records, and his recording of "The House of Blue Lights, became his most successful recording, reaching #9 on the US pop chart. However, his immediate follow-ups, "Hawk-Eye" (written by Boudleaux Bryant) and "Boogie Blues" were less successful. He then recorded more upbeat numbers in New York City with producer Hugo Peretti, including "Bright Red Convertible", "Baby Doll", and his second hit, "The Auctioneer", which reached # 59 on the chart in late 1956.

After being dropped by Mercury, he recorded one unsuccessful album for Imperial Records, Now Hear This! Songs Of The Fighting 40s, before gradually fading into obscurity. Miller moved to Anchorage, Alaska, did a stint playing piano in The Sage Room at Harvey's Lake Tahoe, and later to Maui where he played at The Whale's Tale for many years. He died there in 2000 at the age of 75.

I take you back to that July evening in 1955. Try to visualize pulling up to the Willow Cove Post Office in that 1947 Mercury and hearing the frogs croaking in the nearby swamp and listening to Chuck Miller and the House of Blue Lights for the first time.

Rick Rae is president of Post Citizen Media

CHAPTER SIXTEEN

Here's one from my time in Tennessee where I wrote about the difficulties I had trying to handle my wife's sailboat.

SAILING HARD ON THE EGO

I can't dock my wife's boat!

Three times I tried to glide the thing into its proper place at the Douglas Lake Marina last weekend and three times I failed.

Let me explain just a little. First, this is no ordinary boat.

When the wind is light, power is supplied by the mainsail and the jib. The jib is sometimes replaced by a sail that offers 150 percent of the sall area, called a Genoa, or "Gennv.

First, the motor is used to get out of port and to bring it in, neither of which, I do very well. In fact, I don't do very well under sail either. Second it is not my boat, it is Penny's. Registered in her name, selected by her, captained by her, named by her and operated by her (although paid for by me).

Sailing is something she has done since she was a little girl. Penny was learning about halyards, spars, cleats and things at about the same time as I was learning now to survive in street fights. Penny was raised in relative upper-class surroundings on the lakes and streams of northern Ontario while I was raised in relative poverty in the big city ghetto of Hamilton, a steel town in southern Ontario.

This accident of breeding still shows, particularly when we get on the lake.

Penny's first sailboat was a 13-foot Minifish. I was also allowed to sail it. Next, came a 16-foot Sunfish. I was allowed to take it out as well. Then, she graduated to an 18-foot Victoria. Quickly it was made clear that she was the Captain and I was the mate. It really didn't bother me too much because there wasn't a whole lot of room on the boat and I only went out on it once or twice a year.

This year, however, she acquired the 24-footer and it is a beautiful boat. Room for six, can sleep four, has a sink, a motor, head, stereo, and all the comforts of home. I love it.

As a result I've spent more time on the lake so far this season than all the previous years combined. But it has been very hard on my ego. I still haven't learned to sail very well. It takes quite a bit of skill to learn how to play the wind and get the most out of the boat. There is a very fine line between sailing close-hauled to the wind and getting the absolute maximum performance and getting too close and having the sheets flap around like an awning in a wind-storm, causing you to go backwards.

I haven't learned to do that yet. Not only that, I'm still not sure I know "port' from "starboard,' or what is a shroud and what is a spar, or any one of a dozen other terms that come at me rapid-fire as I take mv turn at the controls (excuse me, I mean the tiller).

Oh, my ego can stand the humiliation when I'm out in the lake and things go awry. Usually, there's just Penny to giggle at my clumsiness. Sometimes the other sailors on Douglas Lake, like Dennis and Julie Jarvis or, Charlie Kidd or LeRoy Dyer can tell that I'm messing up, but my ego can handle that too.

No, the real blow comes as I bring the thing into the marina and all those people are standing around, watching as I attempt to maneuver it to the slip, without crashing the bow pulpit into the dock or catching the shrouds on the roof of the Marina. After three tries, I finally surrender the tiller over to the Captain and she glides it right into place with consummate ease. There's no question who is in command of this boat.

If vou're on the lake and you see a sailboat named "silverheels" going by with a blonde at the helm, you're safe.

If you see a grey-haired guy in the driver's seat, however, better look out, I'm still trying to get through my basic training.

Rick Rae is publisher of The Mountain Press

CHAPTER SEVENTEEN

CALIFORNIA BOUND

A DODGE CHALLENGER IN CAR HEAVEN

After being transferred to LaJolla, California in 1987, I noticed all the classic cars running around on the local roads. It looked like 'car-heaven' to me. All the 50's and 60's cars from my youth seemed to magically appear.

I decided I had to fulfil a fantasy and own a muscle car. A GTO, Barracuda, Challenger, Oldsmobile 442 or something along those lines would meet my needs. So, I went car shopping and found a guy down in El Cahon who had a lot full of collector cars. I was immediately drawn to the 1970 Dodge Challenger. I had always loved the styling of that car and since it was California, it had to be a convertible.

There was a red one with a white leather interior that caught my eye right away. It was powered by the 383 cubic inch V8 (6.3 liter) that was an option that year for the RT model. Generating 335 horsepower, it had a three-speed automatic transmission and featured the famous 'shaker-style' hood. Four different hoods (bonnets) were offered in 1970. The standard hood was almost flat with a molded peak running down the center. The R/T came as standard with the power bulge hood fitted with hood pins (located fore and aft across the hood). This large power bulge really gave the impression of a large engine underneath and contained two air intakes which were not connected directly to the air filter.

Optional was the shaker hood scoop which was mounted directly on the engine intake and stuck up through the hood. The T/A model had a fiberglass hood with a large air intake molded into it which fed directly into the engine.

When we started up the RT, the engine sounded a bit off to me and would not idle well. Sitting alongside was a white convertible sporting a red vinyl interior, powered by a 275 horsepower, 340 cubic inch V8, (5.6 liter) with the same 3-speed torque flite automatic transmission. It started right up and smoothed out with a steady drone from the dual exhausts, that was like music to my ears. And, since it was priced quite a bit lower than the

RT model, it quickly became my favorite, although I liked the power bulge in the hood of the RT model.

The manifold sported a four-barrel carburetor but the seller didn't know if that was stock or had been added by the previous owner. It didn't matter to me as I wasn't worried about fuel economy. A set of Mickey Thompson finned valve covers also appeared to have been installed by the prior owner.

I didn't like the tires that were on the car, so on the way home, I stopped at a tire store and had them mount four Good Years installed on a set of American Racing chrome wheels. I opted to have the chromed spoked inserts installed as I thought the spoked rims and chrome spinners set the car off well.

So, for a little less than I had expected I was now running around the golden state in my beautiful Challenger ragtop. I felt as though I was officially a Californian!

Unfortunately, our time in California was short-lived. The following year, I was moved to be the CEO of a new start-up operation in Albuquerque, New Mexico. Also, a change of corporate policy had been enacted that restricted vehicle transport for executives being relocated just to two.

At the time, we had several vehicles in the household----- The Challenger, a 1988 Chevrolet Suburban that was our horse trailer towing vehicle, a 1987 Suzuki Samurai, a 1988 Mustang convertible, my daughter's 1984 Dodge convertible, and a 1962 Volkswagen project car. That made six in total, or seven if we included the horse trailer. Finally, we decided to load up the horses, hitch the trailer to the Suburban, have my wife drive the Suzuki to Albuquerque and sell all the others.

The Mustang convertible was an easy sell, as was (surprisingly), the Volkswagen, the '84 Dodge was sold at a bit of a loss but the Challenger that appraised at $12,000 in 1988 was a tough sell. I finally left it on a consignment lot with a price tag of ten grand, hoping to break even. After two months the consignment guy told me that the best offer he had was $7,500. Today, that car would bring $175,000 easy. But that was then and this is now and that is the way the car business works. Away went my Challenger.

Rick Rae is vice president of Triple Crown Media Inc.

CHAPTER EIGHTEEN

WHO IS IN CHARGE HERE?

A NEW HORSE OWNER LEARNS PATIENCE

By Rick Rae
Light Publisher

"Some glory in their birth.
Some in their wealth.
Some in their body's force.
Some in their hounds and hawks.
Some in their horse."
William Shakespeare

These words from the immortal Bard are quoted in Robert Vavra's latest tribute to the horse, "Equus Reined." Vavra has written several books accompanied by his excellent photography, dedicated to this noblest of all animals.

As a newcomer to the Wonders of the horse, I too, am finding glory.

The story began last fall.

Sailing was our pastime. So much so that my wife, Penny, towed our sloop all 2,600 miles of the trip from Tennessee to California last October.

Once here, however, sailing the ocean just didn't seem as enjoyable as sailing around the large inland lake we were accustomed to.

Penny decided to pursue an ambition held since early childhood and learn to ride a horse. First came lessons, then a leased horse, then a purchased horse and then, a converted husband. I took over the leased horse and began a once-a-week experience like none other. Once the hook was set, I, too, sought to buy my own horse. My quest was realized with the purchase of a 7-year-old quarter horse, obtained from a Naval officer being transferred to Italy.

The attitude that the buyer {me) was of more concern than the price tipped me off that there was a special relationship between the horse and its owner.

I've since learned that this relationship is something that exists between nearly every horse and rider.

It is very difficult to describe the feeling that comes upon you when riding, grooming or just looking at your horse. The cock of an eyebrow, the tossing of the mane, a steady, trusting stare. The paw of a hoof on the ground...these are all part of the silent transmissions between horse and man.

Sometimes the passage of signals is downright eerie.

Horses are very, very sensitive. A depressed mood or a sudden outburst of anger are immediately relayed to the animal. Minute shifts in weight. Tone of voice or a subtle movement are all signals to the horse that are then picked up and translated into behavior.

As I'm learning this new language to communicate with horses, I'm finding out more about myself. I've never been the calmest person in the world. Emotions can swing quickly from elation to depression. I get up easily and go down just as fast.

My family has learned to live with my behavior, not so, my horse.

An angry rider transmits the aggression, resulting in a nervous horse. Similarly, horses pick up on depression, fear, and the entire gamut of human emotion. Boy, have I learned. After fighting a prancing horse for several hours of an evening ride, the message finally hit home that the horse's actions weren't going to change unless mine changed.

And so, my horse is training me. Little by little, I'm learning a thing called patience...something that raising four kids didn't seem to do. I'm learning to be tolerant, how to suppress anger, how to give praise that is genuine, how to be strict and a host of other things. On top of that, I'm enjoying every minute of it.

I once read something by a long-forgotten author, that every footprint man has made in his journey through civilization has been accompanied by a hoofprint.

I think I'm beginning to understand.

Rick Rae is publisher of the Light newspapers.

CHAPTER NINETEEN

With this column I confess my lack of education to my readers.

OLD DOG LEARNS NEW TRICKS

NEVER TOO OLD TO LEARN

by Rick Rae

For seven years I published a daily newspaper in East Tennessee and wrote a regular weekly column. Here is one that I wrote back in the mid-80's that some folks may find interesting.

Originally published in the Sevier County (TN) Mountain Press on May 2, 1984.

I have gone through some learning experiences recently and would like to share one with you. *"You're never too old to learn"*, seems more appropriate to me than, *"you can't teach an old dog new tricks."*

To provide some background, I'll have to share a secret that most readers of my stuff already suspect. I am a high school dropout. I left school midway in my last year of high school back in 1958. Over the years I've picked up quite a bit of practical knowledge and with a lot of good luck, managed to remain gainfully employed in the ensuing years.

Several months ago, education came up as the main topic at the dinner table in the Rae home and my lack of a high school diploma was a bit of an embarrassment to me with three decent students sitting around the table. A little inner voice suggested that I wasn't providing a very good example for improving grades or staying in school, so I resolved to study up and obtain a high school diploma.

A few weeks ago, I journeyed into the University of Tennessee to take the multi-part exam for the General Educational Development examination. The time allowed for this is six hours and 45 minutes and the subjects include writing skills, social studies, science, reading skills and mathematics.

Instructions were given to me and another young man of about 19 or 20 and the two of us began the ordeal of working against the clock to complete the exams. The first of these was science and as I plodded through the chemistry and physics tests, I began to wonder what I was trying to prove after two decades absence from a classroom. My ego really was crushed when my companion got up and turned in his exam after just 45 minutes of our 90-minute test period had elapsed. I struggled on and managed to finish just before time ran out.

Next, followed social studies and although some of the political science stuff slowed me down, I did manage to complete the task in about the same time as my young companion. Just before lunch we took on mathematics. Now, math has never been my strong suit and as I labored over the geometry and algebra problems, I glanced over to see this young whipper-snapper already on the last few pages, not even using the scratch paper provided for calculations. I already had reams of paper used up and was only halfway finished. Once again, I was alone as he left for lunch, leaving me a good half hour prior to deadline.

As we began the afternoon tests, I was sure I detected a smirk on his face at the nerve of this old gray-haired guy even trying to keep pace.

Writing skills was the lead exam after lunch and I tore into the task with fervor. The time allocated was 75 minutes and I beamed a little as I left the room after 30 minutes to turn in my finished product. It was clear that writing was not this young man's best subject as he used the full amount of time to finish.

Then we were handed the reading and comprehension skills exam as the final task for the day. Twenty minutes later I was finished and felt pretty good about the day's efforts. As I left the building, I noticed my young friend was still working on the early part of the exam with a troubled look on his face. I couldn't help but feel sorry for him.

A few days later I received a call informing me that I had scored extremely well on the exams and would be receiving my diploma shortly.

I hope the young man who shared the day with me gets his as well.

Rick Rae is president of the Post-Citizen Media company.

CHAPTER TWENTY

When I heard that a moonshine museum was being planned to open in Gatlinburg I just had to comment so I wrote this column and submitted to my old newspaper.

HELPING TO FIGHT SEVIER COUNTY UNEMPLOYMENT

THE BENEFITS OF MOONSHINE

The recent news that some folks are planning a Moonshine Museum for Gatlinburg brought back some memories.

Back in the early-1980's, Lamar Alexander, then governor of Tennessee put together a Governor's conference on economic development. He invited representatives of many companies from different countries to come and see what Tennessee had to offer.

The site of the conference was the Opryland Hotel in Nashville, and cities and counties throughout the state were invited to participate with exhibits touting their wares.

At that time I was publisher of the Mountain Press and also a member of the Sevier County Industrial Development Committee. As a group we were concerned about the high unemployment during non-tourism season and we were determined to develop a County industrial park and recruit industry. (That park ultimately came to be as Hodsen-Hicks Industrial Park but that is another story for another time).

We were determined to have Sevier County represented at the Governor's Conference and began making plans for our exhibit. We pulled together a montage of photos showing the features of our area, along with a fifteen-minute narrative and created a presentation to run at our assigned booth on the floor of the auditorium on a continuous basis.

I wasn't convinced that any real business would be conducted on the floor of the conference and suggested that we also book a suite at the hotel to entertain any serious delegates in a more informal surrounding. What I had in mind was a relaxed setting with some comfortable chairs, a buffet and some refreshments.

Some members of the County Commission got wind of my plans for the refreshment part of the deal and were concerned that alcohol may be served. At the next commission meeting it was made very clear to members of the Industrial Development Committee that no County funds would be spent on such nonsense.

With some disappointment, I made my way back from the courthouse to my office across the street (The Mountain Press was located downtown on Court Street at that time), determined to proceed with the suite and have the newspaper foot the bill. Just as I entered, the phone rang and Carmen Townsend, the Sheriff was on the other end.

"Rick, I heard the commission shot you down on your plans tonight", he said. *"But if you want to entertain those folks the right way, I think I have some 'shine' we've confiscated that I can let you have."*

Well, I thanked him for his offer and told him I may drop by the next day to pick some of the stuff up. Just then the phone rang again. This time it was Conley Huskey, then mayor of Pittman Center.

"Rick, that's a sorry thing they did", Conley drawled. *"If you want, I have some 'shine' up here that someone dropped off the other day, you're welcome to pick it up or I could drop it off when I'm down that way"*.

"That's awfully kind of you, Conley", I responded.

You want pints or quarts", he replied.
"That person leave both sizes", I said.
"I believe he did", said Conley.
"You want white or char", he went on.
"Well, maybe a little of both wouldn't hurt", I told him.

Sure enough, the next day I had enough Tennessee home brew to stock up the suite in good fashion.

At the Opryland we had a number of visitors to our exhibit and even more back at our hospitality suite. There we rolled out the Sevier County welcome mat and engaged in some good conversation. Some of our Japanese friends also discovered that in addition to being smooth to drink, the real good 'shine' burns with the prettiest blue flame you ever saw when the lights in the suite were turned down low.

That evening we signed an agreement with the Fuji Valve company from Japan for the very first tenant in our new Industrial Park. We made some good friends that evening.... our presence at the conference was a success. It probably would not have happened without the Moonshine!

Rick Rae retired in 2006 after forty years publishing newspapers. He now owns Continental Features, a supplier of colored comics to newspapers and makes his home in Georgia. He was publisher of the Mountain Press from 1979 to 1987.

CHAPTER TWENTY-ONE

MY MUSTANG GT'S

TURNING A MUSTANG INTO A COBRA

I fell for the Mustang GT back in the early part of 1965 when I worked as a copywriter for Western Tire and Auto located in London, Ontario.

One of the senior buyers for the company had just taken delivery of a brand-new Mustang convertible with all the GT options. This meant his car was equipped with a 271 horsepower V-8, floor mounted 4-speed transmission, quick ratio steering, rally pack gauges including a tachometer and clock. Plus a special handling package that included heavy duty springs front and rear, a rear stabilizer bar, fifteen inch wheels and tires and limited slip differential... all for just $40 more.

This all-black beauty even came with black leather upholstery. He quickly took it to our auto center where the stock mufflers were removed and replaced with Thrush glass-packs had just been added to our accessory line. I fell in love with that car immediately.

My love for the GT remained dormant until one day in 1987 I spotted a new 1988 Mustang GT convertible in a San Diego dealer showroom. This little gem was outfitted with Riken Wheels and tires. It begged me to take it home. We negotiated a trade on my '85 Honda and soon it was in my driveway. With as 0-60 time of 6.8 seconds this GT was no slouch off the line. By now the 302 ci was still rated at a modest 225 horsepower, still haunted by the runaway horsepower claims of the seventies muscle cars.

One thing that bothered me about the GT was the way the exhaust pipes exited the back end of the car. In their wisdom, the engineers at Ford had turned down the ends of the exhaust pipes so they exited under the rear bumper. I thought that looked ugly.

So, I had a muffler shop cut back the pipes and weld on three-inch diameter extensions, cut through the bumper cover and extend the exhaust pipes out where they could be seen. Now my

GT looked like it belonged. The interior of the car was decked out in red vinyl and looked pretty spiffy.

Then we advance to 1996 when the GMC Conversion van I had been driving bit the dust and put me in the market for another car. I found a 1995 Mustang GT convertible on a lot in Winder, Georgia that had been owed by the business manager of the dealership. I quickly made a deal on this little sweetheart that was painted in Wimbleton white with a red vinyl interior. It sported the 5.0 (302 ci) High output V-8 that was rated at 240 hp.

I was not content to leave this as just a plain GT. I wanted to make it into a Cobra. The '95 Cobra had the same basic 5.0 engine but it was rated at 305 hp. As I began to make my Cobra clone I changed the badging on the car by adding SVT (special vehicle technology) logos to the rear and the Cobra snake emblem on the front fenders and grille, replacing the Mustang identification.

Next came fully chromed Cobra wheels, a Cobra rear bumper cover and Cobra tailight and parking light covers. Then I addressed the engine. I changed the exhaust system by installing Flowmaster headers and stainless steel 2-1/2 inch pipes. Then added a cold air intake system, installed larger diameter fuel injectors and had a tuner shop re-flash the computer to take into account these changes.. A reinforcing strut was added tieing the shock towers together to make certain the increased torque could be handled without twisting the engine on its mounts.

Then I visited an upholstery shop for a new top and real leather seats in bright red soft leather. The stock sound system was upgraded to Ford's Premium system with 500 watts.

My Mustang was equipped with a 4-speed automatic overdrive transmission (AOD) that came stock with an anemic 2:73 rear axle ratio. While visiting a Mustang performance shop one day they talked me into pulling out the stock differential and replacing it with a limited slip 3:73 rear axle. This lower gear ratio (higher numerically) woke the car up immediately. Although gas mileage suffered, the increase in performance was noticeable and my Cobra clone was complete.

Rick Rae is Publisher of the Citizen Newspapers

CHAPTER TWENTY-TWO

I began to look at some old columns from Tennessee while researching the previous column and ran across this one I wrote about our rafting trip down the Chatooga River of Georgia/North Carolina fame.

RIVER RAFTING WHERE DELIVERANCE LEFT OFF.

CHALLENGING THE CHATOOGA

The word "Macho" springs from the Spanish word for masculine but in the past decade it has come to mean much more than that. It is THE word to describe virile, courageous, adventurous MEN.

Mental images of Macho are implanted within our minds and red-blooded American males identify with them quickly in spirit, if not in the flesh, Marlon Brando astride a Triumph motorcycle in the movie "The Wild One' Steve McQueen driving a super-fast Mustang in "Bullitt". Or how about the Macho of Clint Eastwood as a nameless gunfighter or in later movies as "Dirty Harry", or a bare knuckles boxer.

All of these images have been identified with by millions of men as they ride their Hondas, accelerate quickly in the family car or just sit back by the television and fantasize. Some identify well with Burt Reynolds and the sales of black Trans-Am automobiles is testimony to the success of his power in the "Smokey and the Bandit" movies. I identify with Reynolds in another role. Who could forget the terror of the weekend river rafting trip as Burt Reynolds, John Voight, Ned Beatty and Ronny Cox took that fateful trip down the rapids of the Chatooga river?

What man could not identify with Reynolds, biceps bulging over the life jacket, muscles rippling as he and his crew dug paddles in to steady the raft as it hurtled down the rapids?

And so, on a weekend in June my fantasy became reality.

"We're going down the Chatooga, you know, the river they filmed 'Deliverance' on. Want to go?" The speaker was Brent Blalock, local contractor, himself a macho kind of guy, *"It's a great time,"* chimed in Lynn Webb, local car dealer. *"we've never lost anyone yet."*

Not wanting to appear any less macho than these two guys I agreed to go along, but deep down inside I had visions of the body that washed down the rocks in the movie.

Our group assembled late one afternoon at McNelly-Whaley Motors to begin our adventure. I was there first and as each member of our group gathered, I found that all had previous experience at river rafting. Just as the "Magnificent Seven' men that Yul Brynner assembled each had their special brand of macho, so did each member of our group.

The previously mentioned Blalock and Webb, big, tough guys. Then Bill Carroll, the banker, another six foot, two hundred plus pounder. Next, Ron Grove of Arnold Engineering, not as big as the others, but lithe and muscular just the same. We were joined by Ben Brabson, a local attorney and the group began to recount tales of prior adventures. Brabson's shrewd navigational instincts were legendary, it seemed and added yet another skill to the group.

As we waited for the seventh member to arrive, I was beginning to have second thoughts about my presence. Number seven turned out to be local insurance broker, Coyle Fox, and my spirits soared as I discovered that Coyle was also a first-timer.

We all piled into the van and headed for South Carolina. Our destination was Dillard, Georgia just a short distance from the Wildwater Ltd. headquarters on the Chatooga River. Wildwater runs trips on the Chattooga as well as on the Ocoee and Nolichucky Rivers in Tennessee.

My traveling companions continued to tell the tales of previous trips and caught the attention of Coyle and myself with talk of a sacrifice to the river god. Brabson, in particular, held forth that the trip would be a bad one unless the river god had a sacrifice early on. It wouldn't be painful, he assured us, just out of the raft and into the rapids. Naturally, either Coyle or Rae were earmarked to be sacrifices.

That evening we feasted at the Dillard house and read the brochures of the upcoming trip, One section of the rapids did little for my appetite that evening. It was called "The Last Supper." The Chatooga is divided into four sections. Section three is the Deliverance trip, where most of the filming took place and I assumed that was our destination. My heart did a flip-flop when I discovered that Webb had reserved us on section Four, which begins where the Deliverance trip ends. This part is called "the Ultimate Challenge" and covers the steepest section of river being run on a commercial basis in the Eastern United States!

"Great," I thought, *"if I'm going to go it might as well be on the Ultimate Challenge."*

Since sleep was going to be difficult, we gathered in Lynn Webb's room for a bedtime beverage of warm milk and the boys took pity on my first time by letting me win at a few hands of 'Old Maid'.

The sun had not had a chance to burn off the morning dew as we were up and headed for the river. *"No turning back now,"* I thought. I hoped that my wife could locate the will and insurance policies.

Our guide, Jobe gave us the rundown of how to respond to his commands on the river and instructed us on the technique to use in case you went out of the raft. Brent and Ben both prodded me and told me to listen well to Jobe's advice.

"It's sure nice to have the confidence of your shipmates," I pondered.

We pushed the raft into the river and caught the current going downstream. It had rained the night before and the river was running strong. The white foam that curled around the rocks did little to calm me. Suddenly, we were swirling down a small waterfall! One minute the river was there and the next it just dropped off and down.

"Paddle hard," shouted Jobe. *"Back left."* came his command as we bounced over a hidden rock, and suddenly Ben Brabson catapulted out of the raft. Ben was dragged under by the current and popped up just in front of us.

Ben's experience took over as he laid back and let the river take him to an eddy of calm water where Jobe pulled Ben back aboard. After assuring ourselves that Ben was okay. we all breathed a sigh of relief. The river god had had his sacrifice. It would be a safe trip.

I'm still not certain if the crafty Brabson hadn't planned it that way all along.

Now the challenges came faster and faster-- Raven Rock Rapids, where the form of a raven can be seen etched in the face of the cliff, seven-foot falls, where the drop is accompanied by a hard turn to the left which fills the raft with water as it hits the bottom and stalls in the turn. Down through the Corkscrew, past Decapitation rock, which derives its name from what it will do to you if you don't get down when going through.

Finally, we drop down through Jawbone and Sock-Em-Dog before beaching on a sandy inlet for lunch. Lunch has been bouncing up and down in the front of our raft in a waterproof container and our crew makes short work of it.

Six hours after we began, we make the final drop into Lake Tugaloo and begin our paddle to the exit point. After cooling off with a dip in the lake. Our spirits are high. We have challenged Chatooga and won!

The Sevier County River Rafting Association now has two new members.

We're now ready for our next expedition, which is planned for July on the Nolichucky. It's challenging, it's fun and yes, it's dangerous. The danger, however, is only what you wish. Not everyone has to run "the Ultimate Challenge."

There are trips available for anyone, ages six and up, on such rivers as the Nanthahala, the French Broad, the Ocoee, the Nolichucky and, of course the Chatooga.

Move over Burt and Clint. Make room for some new members.

Rick is publisher of the Mountain Press

CHAPTER TWENTY-THREE

Here is a column I wrote in May, 1996 the month after we settled in Georgia.

EVENTFUL JOURNEY TO GEORGIA

FIRST COLUMN FROM A NEW PUBLISHER

Now that my wife and I have finally moved to our new home in Georgia I thought it might be appropriate to put a column together. From time to time I will write a column based on personal experiences to share with readers. I've been around the business long enough to know that I don't qualify as a journalist, so that is one of the reasons you won't see my byline on a regular basis.

We had an eventful trip from Pennsylvania last weekend with me driving the van, packed to the max with two dogs, towing our horse trailer, also loaded full of tack as well as one appaloosa and one quarter horse. My wife, Penny had her little car loaded to the rooftop and barely had enough room for her. We kept in touch with the CB radios to pass the time and to keep me awake.

Just as we approached Fairmont, W. Va., in a driving rainstorm, the right rear tire on our van blew apart. Trying to keep the trailer upright with over a ton of horses, while fighting to keep from plowing over a steep hill was very intense. When I finally wrestled the rig to a stop, we discovered that the steepness of the hill plus the weight of the horse trailer prevented me from getting the jack under the truck. Since we didn't have enough room to unload the horses safely with heavy traffic whizzing by at high speed, I decided to take Penny's car, head for town and find help.

I tracked the wrecker driver down at a cafe where he was having a leisurely breakfast. *"U'll be along directly,"* he drawled, *"jes go back tuh the interstate and wait fer me."* I did as instructed but "directly" turned out to be an hour and a half. He got the rig jacked up and mounted the spare but since the tire was destroyed, I decided to seek out a tire store and replace it before resuming our journey.

It was now after noon, and I quickly discovered that two of the three tire stores in Fairmont, W. Va., close at noon. The third closed at one o'clock and was across town, so we hightailed it through the noon traffic and arrived 10 minutes before closing. I bought one tire at the price two would cost in most places and we were back on the road.

By the time we unloaded the horses at a friend's stable in Knoxville they had been in the trailer for 13 hours, which is a long time for our guys. They were pretty happy to stretch their legs. On Sunday, we finished the journey and on Monday our furniture arrived. So now we're knee deep in boxes and wrapping paper as we try to put our household back together again. Soon all will be normal once more.

Some folks have asked me if there will be any changes to the newspaper, or what our editorial policy is. I will share my response. Our corporate owners at Gray Communications have a very simple philosophy, which appeals to me. Very simply, our newspapers will reflect the values of the communities they serve.

As I have traveled the area I have been asked some other questions and I'll try to address them as well.

What are the politics of the newspaper? We have no political agenda. I tend to be a bit on the conservative side, but generally our papers will lean towards whatever or whomever will benefit the overall needs of the community regardless of political affiliation.

Who decides what runs in the newspaper? That job belongs to the editor of the newspaper. Alice Queen is fully qualified to make the news judgments required to make certain we have a readable, local paper that reflects the communities it serves.

Why do you continue to run that Friday Phone Poll? We recently asked our readers to give us their opinion of the Phone Poll, and those who responded were overwhelmingly in favor of it. Some took us to task for allowing anonymous cheap shots at folks in leadership positions, but as long as they are not libeling any person, we feel that kind of goes with the territory of being in a public position.

Well, that's all we have room for today, I'll sign off and leave room for some interesting stuff.

Rick Rae is publisher of The Rockdale Citizen and The Gwinnett Daily Post.

CHAPTER TWENTY-FOUR

This car was a genuine impulse buy. I saw the soft mint green machine on the showroom floor and just had to own it.

THE MITSUBISHI PROJECT

HOPPING UP A V-6

It was spring 2003 and the 1995 Mustang convertible I was driving was beginning to give me some problems. In the latter part of 2002 I had done some work on the five-liter engine to up the performance by installing larger fuel injectors, a cold air kit, and higher gearing in the rear axle, all in the hopes of bumping the horsepower and torque closer to the numbers produced by the same engine that was installed in the Cobra version of the same car.

Unfortunately, all that effort put additional strain on the engine that manifested itself with problems due to overheating and strain on the transmission. As a result, I was faced with spending more money on upgrades.

While visiting one of our car dealer advertisers one day I saw a beautiful little convertible in his showroom that caught my eye. It was a soft light green color and was badged as an Eclipse, Spyder GTS... I had to have it!

After a quick appraisal of my Mustang and a couple of hours of negotiating, I left the dealership in my new ride. The 3.0 liter V-6 put out 210 horsepower but it didn't quite have the snap that I was used to from my Mustang. I decided to go and visit a tuner shop that specialized in Japanese cars to see what we could do to improve performance. The next month saw me leaving the Spyder in their shop for many modifications.

First off, they turbocharged the V-6, to drive more charged air into the combustion chambers. Then they increased the size of the injector nozzles from 14 millimeter to 17 in order to push more gasoline into the throttle body. Then the Spyder went to an exhaust specialist to have headers fabricated that dumped out into a two-inch diameter stainless steel system with dual pipes running front to back. A gauge pod was installed on the driver's side A pillar to monitor oil and manifold pressure. Then they had to change out the CV front Axle assembly to install a heavier weight unit able to handle the increased horsepower and torque.

When the project was completed, the engine generated about 305 horsepower on the dynamometer which was comparable with what I was getting from the 5.0 liter V-8 in my Mustang. This was a pretty fast little Spyder and left many so-called muscle car drivers scratching their heads as I left them choking in rubber dust.

Rick Rae is president of Post Citizen Media

CHAPTER TWENTY-FIVE

THE OLDSMOBILE PROJECT

RESTORING A CLASSIC

In mid-September of 1972 I was transferred from the Winnipeg Tribune to the company's newly acquired newspaper in Windsor, Ontario. This was a pleasant surprise as we hated living in Winnipeg.

A month earlier we had returned from a vacation to the southern USA and I announced that I wished to leave and find work in a warmer climate.

At first, I was ignored but then someone at the head office apparently took notice and an equivalent position was created for me at their new newspaper, located at the southern-most point in Canada.

Windsor was just across the river from Detroit, the motor city. The cars that were on the road in that area were gorgeous looking and sweet-sounding to a motor-head like me. 1972 was almost the end of the muscle-car era, but there were still many hot cars on the road. 1972 was the year an Oldsmobile 442 convertible was selected as the Indianapolis 500 pace car.

The top-of-the-line 442 (4-on-the-floor, 4-barrel carburetor, dual exhaust), was the ultimate muscle car, based on that year's Cutlass Supreme. I loved the style of that car.

Since I was driving an eight-year old Chevy at the time, I was a long way removed from owning a 1972 Cutlass Supreme but that car stuck in my mind and I was determined to own one someday.

Fast forward twenty years to Loganville, Georgia where I worked as president and publisher of two daily newspapers in the Atlanta area and drove a 1992 Cadillac STS. I still lusted after the Oldsmobile Cutlass Supreme convertible and earnestly began to search for one.

I turned up a rust-free, low mileage Cutlass in southern Alabama and brought it back to Georgia. The car was very straight and had just been re-painted in Saturn gold metallic, the interior had been redone with bucket seats upholstered in what was called Moroccan vinyl. What was questionable was the engine. The 5.7 liter (350 cubic inch) original, not to be confused with the Chevy 350 of the same year, sounded a bit sick. We pulled the engine and sent it off to a quality rebuilder.

While waiting on the engine, I scoured the junkyards in search of some of the little things to complete my Olds project.

I found a set of original wheels and chrome trim rings in a yard in Gratis, Georgia, along with hood inserts that I had chromed at a local shop. I finally found a set of 442 trumpet-style exhaust tips at a yard in Lawrenceville and quickly snapped them up. Then $2,500 later the engine was back in the car with pleasant sounds burbling through its twin glass-packs.

I was cautioned to gingerly break in this engine by keeping it at a steady low rev range for the first 2,000 miles or so. But the throaty sound of that engine led me astray. I just could not resist blipping the pedal every time someone in a performance car rolled up beside me.

I was on the way back from a car show in Pigeon Forge Tennessee when a guy in an SS 396 Chevelle ran up alongside and the challenge was met. I watched as my tachometer climbed up way past the red line and then heard the 'clank' as one of the bearings let loose in the bottom end of the engine in my pretty little Cutlass.

It was a long, lonely ride home as a passenger in the tow truck.

Rick Rae is president of The Mountain Press

CHAPTER TWENTY-SIX

CAR SONGS

LOVING THE MUSIC ABOUT CARS

I love songs about cars. Ever since I first heard Maybelline and then Rocket 88, I thirsted for more songs about cars and I wasn't disappointed.

As the sixties arrived we had the Beach Boys with Fun, Fun, Fun, 409, Little Deuce Coupe, Shut Down and others. Jan and Dean ran with Dead Man's Curve, Drag City and the Little Old Lady from Pasedena. The Rip Chords chimed in with Hey, Little

Cobra followed by Ronnie and the Daytonas with Little GTO and even Wilson Pickett had a ride with Mustang Sally. And who could forget Paul Revere and the Raiders with SS 396?.

I have collected many, many songs about cars and hot rods from obscure groups over the years. You may have never heard of the Duals, The Routers, The Shutdowns, Stickshifters, Quartermilers or the Gran Prixx but each of them did great cars songs. Even more mainstream groups added in a car song or two like, Bob Dylan with From a Buick 6, Bob Seger with Makin' Thunderbirds, the Who with Bucket T and John Fogerty with Hot Rod Heart.

Two rare and more obscure cars songs came from the aforementioned Gran Prixx and Ronnie and the Daytonas.

The Gran Prixx piece is called '41 Ford and takes me back to high school days of 1955-56. There was a senior at my school who had a '41 Ford coupe that was so beautiful it could make you cry. In the years that car motored around the school it was never painted. It was finished in Gray primer and the body had been 'Channeled' and the top had been 'Chopped'. Channeling means to remove the body and re-install it so it sits lower on the frame. Chopping mean to cut a section out of the body of one to two inches and then weld it back together and fill the seams. That '41 sat so low and looked so cool!!! The engine was a V-8 Flathead that had been 'stroked' and 'bored'. What started out at 241 cubic inches was opened up to about 300 cubic inches by lengthening the connecting rods (stroking) to increase the stroke of the pistons and routing out the cylinders (boring) so that oversize pistons could be installed. Both of these actions bumped up the torque and horsepower.

The sound of that engine rumbling out of the headers and into the twin glasspacked mufflers stays with me today. There were no catalytic converters to get in the way of the flow out the pipes back in those days!

The Daytona's song honors the '32 Studebaker Dictator Coupe. This was a rare piece of iron that came out of South Bend, Indiana as opposed to Detroit. It was a beautiful slope-backed coupe that featured side mounts and a rumble seat. Powered by a 337 cubic inch straight eight engine, the Dictator put out 135 horsepower and in the early 30's that meant performance with a capital P. The song doesn't mention any modifications to the car but even stock, it could outrun many cars from the 40's and 50's. It reminds me a bit of the straight eight that powered my friend, Don Morrison's '38 Buick Special that left a lot of 50's cars in the dust. Don's '38 had triple carbs, installed at the factory and was a very early muscle car.

Studebaker made Commanders, Presidents and Dictators but wisely dropped the name Dictator later in the 30's as Hitler and Mussolini rose to power.

Kids today don't care about cars like we did. The magic that we enjoyed is lost forever. A friend of mine said he tried get his kids interested in Lucas' American Graffiti the other evening and they found it boring...."*Too many cars and no action*", they said.

Rick Rae is president of Post Citizen Media

CHAPTER TWENTY-SEVEN

NOT EVERY STORY IS WORTH THE COST

FACING A DILEMMA IN WEST VIRGINIA

For a short time I was publisher of the Journal in Martinsburg, WV. I wrote this editorial because I felt strongly that every story does not need to be published immediately.

By Richard Rae
The (Martinsburg) Morning Journal

Not Every Story Is Worth the Cost

Several months ago we were alerted that federal, state and local officials were working on a project spearheaded by U.S. Sen. Jay Rockefeller, D-W.Va., to bring an aircraft manufacturing facility to Martinsburg which could employ about 1,300 people.

We elected to hold the story to avoid a bidding war with other areas while private negotiations continued. We agreed to this as we have done in the past and most probably will do in the future.

We're in the business of reporting the news, but we're not in the business of tipping corporate secrets when it could drive away the prospects of 1,300 jobs coming to our area.

We make no apology for caring about the security of your jobs and providing for the potential employment of your children, friends and relatives. We come down on the side of jobs first!

Unfortunately, there are some journalists who believe that news is news and it has to be published no matter what the cost. Last week the Hagerstown, Md., Morning Herald made a bad decision –– a decision which is not in the best interests of the local economy.

It has long been the policy of The Journal to work with officials who strive to move employers to this region. If there were a legitimate reason not to locate such a facility here, we certainly would be the first to say so. There was no reason to print a story that could cost us 1,300 jobs –– or even 50 jobs!

Each newspaper has a constitutional right to publish whatever it wishes. If The Morning Herald wants to foul its own economy, that's one thing. When it crosses the state line and begins to foul ours, that is yet another issue. We do not agree with their news philosophy. There are times when restraint has superior value. This is one of those times.

We hope Swearingen Engineering and Technology Inc. doesn't judge folks in the Eastern Panhandle of West Virginia based on the actions of an out-of-state newspaper which can't hold its water overnight.

CHAPTER TWENTY-EIGHT

This column ran in the Light newspapers...a group of papers that I published in California on September 15, 1988. The thoughts I shared are similar to those shared by the editor of the Mountain Press almost a decade earlier in Tennessee.

NEWSPAPERS CAN BE FAIR AND 'TAKE A STAND' AT SAME TIME

By RICK RAE
Light Publisher

This column is prompted by recent correspondence I've had with a former reader of The Light. I say "former" because the reader took exception to a recent column written by our editor, Mark Stadler, calling for a ban on smoking in the seating area at San Diego Jack Murphy Stadium.

A note on our subscription renewal notice indicated that such views would not be supported by a payment.

Now, I hate to lose a subscriber and I felt obligated to correspond in order to point out the difference between an editorial and a column as well as encourage the reader to submit an opinion of her own, since it was obvious she felt strongly about the smoking issue.

I failed miserably.

A second communication indicated that the point was missed entirely, so I thought I'd try to communicate some information about our business and the difference between "facts" and "opinions."

There aren't many hard and fast rules in the news business. Though the packages may look similar each week, the content of our products is manufactured from scratch every issue. The information comes in, and then we make on-the-spot decisions under deadline pressure about what goes where.

We must be flexible, for relativity is everything. You do one thing this week, another the next. A story planned for page one may have to be bumped to the inside because something more interesting or important has developed.

But we don't play it entirely fast and loose. We follow the basic standards of ethical journalism that have evolved over the years, and we have our own policies to which each staff writer is expected to adhere.

For a newspaper to command the respect of its community, it must project a sense of fair play, and yet be willing to "take a stand" for the good of the community. Sometimes these basic principles conflict with one another. How can we give fair and equal coverage to both sides of a controversial issue and still "take a stand"?

I'm going to delve into this tricky area of "fact" and "opinion" with this list of thoughts:

1. A ban on smoking at Jack Murphy Stadium has been proposed. That is a fact.
2. Whether that action is bad or good is a matter of opinion.
3. If a stadium board member says the ban is good, that is his opinion. If the board member states this view in public or to a reporter, it becomes fact that this member holds a certain opinion.
4. If another board member says the ban is bad, then for the medium to factually report on the issue, both opinions must be printed or aired.

That's what our news pages are all about. Although we didn't report on the above subject since it really wasn't an issue of local importance, one of our staffers did feel strongly enough about the issue to offer an opinion, and that is what the page you're reading now is all about:

- Our opinion. This is where we take a stand on issues. We offer our reasoned judgments as to proper courses of action that we believe will benefit the community. When you see an editorial on the left side of this page it represents the viewpoint of our newspaper as written by our editor. Since it is the paper's point of view it is unsigned, but generally the editorials are authored by Mark Stadler.

- My opinion. You are reading my opinion now. Although it is a matter of semantics, the articles produced by David Dreiman, Al Strolein and other regular contributors are not editorials, they are columns. At times, members of our staff such as Mark or myself also contribute columns for this page, and such columns carry a byline indicating these are individual views. In the case of Mark's recent column about smoking in the stadium, I must say I agree with him, but for another viewpoint look at news editor Kurt Kidman's column today (elsewhere on this page).

- Your opinion. In my opinion, your opinions expressed in letters to the editor are the most important reports our newspapers carry. Over the past few years we have seen a dramatic increase in the number of letters to the editor, and that is terrific. This page is a public forum open to all who want to express their views. It is yours to use and hopefully our former reader may even exercise her right to let us know her views.

CHAPTER TWENTY-NINE

This column from March, 2006 Three months before I retired. It is pretty clear I was upset when I wrote this.

DOES ANYBODY REALLY CARE?

I have been in the media business since 1965 when I took my first job in advertising sales at the Spectator, the daily newspaper in my hometown of Hamilton, Ontario, Canada. I never began to get an appreciation for the journalism side of the business until I joined the management staff of the Oakland Press in Pontiac, Mich., about 10 years later.

That was 1975 and a lot was happening in the news business. Woodward and Bernstein had become household names from unraveling the Watergate story. Ben Bradlee, the managing editor of the Washington Post was portrayed by Jason Robarts as a journalistic icon, and everywhere students wanted to attend journalism school and uncover the big story.

We've come a long way since then, but journalistically, my profession has gone downhill. The portrayal of reporters by television and movie writers hasn't helped us much. We have changed from the heroes of "Lou Grant" to an endless parade of actors who portrayed us as insensitive, uncaring boors with no moral compass. I don't know when it began, but the idiot reporter who was Bruce Willis' adversary in the first "Die Hard" film didn't help. Then we had Sally Field, weaving her web of deceit against Paul Newman in "Absence of Malice," and that led to "Network," where the news had changed so much to entertainment that Faye Dunaway's character says, "All I want out of life is a 20 share and a 30 rating."

And now I'm watching as the fiction turns to real life. I am one of those who believe that the recent sniper attacks may have been accelerated by the media coverage. Even when there was nothing to report, on came the "experts" and "talking heads" to expound on the situation. No wonder the public's opinion of the media is at an all time low. Remember Elian? Jon Benet?

We are just a small local newspaper, but we get tarred with the same brush as the TV news know-nothings (or know-everythings), the Letterman monologues, the Van Susterens and the Courics of the world.

Because of this there are fewer people who really care about what we do than there were 25 years ago. And fewer still believe that there is anything really essential about the filtering and editing of information that we perform.

We've made it much easier for the reader/listener to ignore us because most believe that all voices are created equal – that a blowhard on talk radio has the same credibility as a bureau chief for The Associated Press; and that a bunch of opinions dumped on a Web site has the same depth of research as a story written by a reporter who knows the players and is reviewed by an editor who knows the topic.

And that is scary because it means we may lose even more credibility and more readership as truth, fact and reliability that seemed relatively straightforward 25 years ago, now seem to be thrown aside for garbage. It may be more entertaining, but it's still garbage.

We have an obligation not just to inform but to serve as a check on government and other institutions as set out in the Constitution. Some of that stuff may not be exciting to today's crop of journalism students, but without someone to watch over the shoulders of those charged with the public trust, I am worried about where we may end up.

I believe that there are still folks out there who are looking for meaningful information filtered and edited in a way that is trustworthy and fair. Hopefully, those who hold the nation's institutions accountable will always find people wanting to read and listen.

Rick Rae is publisher of the Rockdale and Newton Citizen newspapers.

CHAPTER THIRTY

IS MEDIA PART OF THE PROBLEM

THE TRAUMA OF ANOTHER SCHOOL SHOOTING

Friday morning I stopped at a local convenience store to pick up copies of USA Today and the Atlanta papers to review their coverage of the Heritage High School shootings here in Conyers.

I had already made an early morning run to our production facility to obtain copies of the Gwinnett Daily Post and the special morning issue of its sister paper the Rockdale Citizen

As I paid the young lady behind the counter, who seemed to be a student herself, she looked at the headlines and questioned, "Why do they keep doing this?"

"The shootings", I responded. "No, she replied, "the publicity, the stories. Why can't they just leave it alone?"

"Well it is a pretty big news story"..., I started, but stopped when it became clear she wasn't interested in debating the topic and had moved on to another customer.

Here comments stayed with me as I returned to the office to read all the material I had collected and do some channel surfing for updates from local television commentators.

It is clear there are parallels to the Conyers and Littleton shootings. It is also clear that the planning, forethought and outcome of the Conyers tragedy was note on the same scale as Littleton.

As president of a communications division overseeing two newspapers and a local television outlet, I am faced with the fact that our actions could add fuel to the fires.

Does our coverage somehow make the perpetrator a hero in the eyes of some misguided youngsters? Does his moment of infamy give rise to thoughts of repetition in their minds so that they too, gain recognition?

I don't think so, but when I use the collective "we" to include all media, I am troubled.

The frenzy that began yesterday morning saw television and radio stations from the southeastern USA gathering in front of Heritage High's field house. Then came the networks on the scene. 20/20, CNN, Fox, and then calls and demands from other news organizations and magazine for copies of our stories and our photos. One organization wanted our photos to re-sell to various supermarket tabloids. Alice Queen, our editor told them to forget about it. Another Major organization attempted to bribe our receptionist into stealing our photographer's negatives for them.

Alice and city editor Chris Starrs made another judgement call that should be noted. The name of the juvenile allegedly responsible for the shootings was not published.

Leslie McCoy news editor of our Gwinnett News and Entertainment Television outlet also ruled against releasing the name but it could be they are a bit gun shy after the Richard Jewell incident.

The teen gunman's name was used in local television and radio reports and some other newspapers including our own Gwinnett Daily Post. J.K. Murphy, editor of the Post decided to use the name for three reasons:

- The name of the juvenile was released in the Columbine shootings.
- The associated Press and other news organizations released the name by the time the Gwinnett paper went to press.
- Local TV and radio were already using the name.

Gary Boley, publisher of the Herald, our sister paper in Albany told me he did not publish the name but felt they could have. Gary's reason was that juvenile law was never intended for actions of this scope and once a Juvenile steps into a larger arena his identity is fair game.

So, what is the correct call? I think it depends on the community in which we operate. This is a small community and everyone who needs to know the name of the individual already knows it. Why take things any further?

The Gwinnett decisions are judgement calls. Gwinnett is sufficiently removed from Rockdale it moves beyond a local story. But why give this kid any recognition whatsoever?

To respond to the convenience clerk's question...we just can't leave it alone. It happened and the story will run its course. I hope it is soon over and the networks and newsmagazines will soon give us back our community.

Rick Rae is president of the Gray communications systems divisions operating the Gwinnett Daily Post, The Rockdale Citizen and Gwinnett News and Entertainment Television

CHAPTER THIRTY-ONE

GROWTH IN ROCKDALE COUNTY

PLANNING FOR THE OLYMPICS

This column ran in the Citizen back in June, 1996 and centered on our newspaper's expansion plans plus a look at the planning for the upcoming Olympics.

Back in March of this year, our management group began to develop short and long range plans for The Citizen. Those involved at the time were me; our editor, Alice Queen; financial director, Susan Colmar; circulation director, Jim Brumbelow; Advertising director, Ernie Yarbrough and production director, Jeff Norris. These six were the key executives at the newspaper.

Much of our plan involved pretty mundane stuff that would excite only newspaper people like us but some courses of action we decided on will impact our readers and advertisers and I thought it would be appropriate to share what's ahead.

First, we discussed the upcoming Olympic games and the impact visitors would have on our newspaper operations. One concern was our press time which starts each weekday at 11:15 am. We try to have all of our papers home delivered by late afternoon. "How", we asked ourselves, "are we going to do this in the midst of massive traffic predicted for our area?"

After much review we decided to alter the publication of the paper from a morning to an afternoon cycle for this period. Thus, as of Monday July 22, the Citizen will be produced in the evening and printed sometime in the early morning hours so distribution can be completed before most folks are out of bed in the morning. That should give us the jump on traffic we need to bring readers the news they have come to expect. If we didn't do this our fear was that papers would not be delivered until late evening and the hardship and safety of our carriers would be a concern.

We hope that customers and employees will understand the need to make the change and that moving things topsy-turvy will just be short-term until the Olympics have ended in early October.

We then discussed the need for us to provide coverage of events on the weekend as a wrap-up for the weekday activities. Many stories, not just about the games, will need coverage about the impact everything will have on our community. We decided the only way we could accomplish that would be to print a Saturday edition. So, starting Saturday, July 20, we will publish a weekend newspaper.

We like that idea so much that we did a small amount of research and discovered we aren't the only ones who think it is a good idea. So, we will keep the Saturday publication going even after the Olympic games are history. There is enough news and information around the county to support such a publication and more timely presentation of things such as Friday night local sports is sure to be welcomed.

Also, in early June I got a call from the publisher from Westdeutsche Allgermeine Zeitung (WAZ), a daily newspaper in Essen, Germany asking for our help in producing a special German language newspaper, during the Olympics. He wanted it printed and distributed daily to the Olympic delegations from Germany, Austria and surrounding countries who would be visiting or participating in the events.

This 16-page newspaper would contain eight pages transmitted to our computers in Georgia, produced from Germany plus eight more pages that would be produced locally using our production and delivery staff. We quickly negotiated a contract for this work and put this product into our plan.

I really wanted to produce the official Olympic magazine for the events but the initial meeting I had with the folks at the Atlanta Committee for the Olympic Games (ACOG) killed that idea. Then, I proposed that they let us be the official newspaper for the events at the Georgia International Horse Park. I promised that we would alter our distribution schedule, change our delivery times, add the Saturday edition needed to provide the Order of Go for weekend events and handle all distribution on buses going to and from the events.

I was elated when they agreed to this proposal.

I also wanted to make certain our key advertisers got to enjoy the Olympic events but that idea did not work out. When I arrived in Georgia to take over Citizen operations in March, 1996, Olympic plans were already in full swing. In looking over some stuff left by the guy I replaced I found a note about four Olympic ticket packages that the company had paid nine thousand dollars for that we could not afford. The payment was made by check to an individual, not a company and I could find no receipt...all I had was a copy of the cancelled check and a guy's name who lived in Atlanta.

I tried to track the guy down but all I could get was a cell phone number that was always on voice mail. *"This is Chuck, I'll call you back."* But, of course, he never did. Finally, I hired a detective to track him down.

We threatened to bring in the authorities (GBI) and that got a response. He told us that the deal made to my predecessor was that the tickets were the real deal but that the tickets themselves could not be delivered until just two days before the events took place.

That killed any thoughts I had to invite advertisers as we couldn't very well invite them at the last minute. Despite that, I pressed him to get them to me quickly.

Finally, the second week in July, he agreed to meet me at a shopping center in east Atlanta and gave me the ticket packages, much too late to do us any good.

Months later the story broke that several local and state politicians had been given ticket packages by Olympic organizers that they then sold to ticket scalpers like Chuck for hundreds of dollars, that were then re-sold for thousands. Like some others, we were scammed.

Rick Rae is president of Post-Citizen Media

CHAPTER THIRTY-TWO

NEW GROWTH WARRANTS NEW PUBLISHER

This column published in the Daily Post on the
last day of December, 1997

Last week, we announced the promotion of Leo Pieri to the
position of publisher of the newspaper. Most folks outside of
our industry don't know exactly What a publisher does, so I
thought would offer a bit of explanation.

If you remember the old TV series, "Lou Grant.", you'll recall
that Lou reported to the editor, Charlie Hume, and Charlie's
boss was the publisher, Mrs. Pinchon.

Now Mrs. Pinchon was a crusty lady who ran the Los Angeles
Tribune with an iron fist and essentially, she was the top
dog involved in all decisions relating to the operations of the
newspaper. Here at the Daily Post, Howard Reed is our Lou
Grant and Norman Baggs is our Charlie Hume. Up until now, I
have been our Mrs. Pinchon but I now pass that responsibility
along to Leo.

Basically, the Publisher acts as a general Manager, making certain that the news, advertising and production departments of the newspaper all interact smoothly. The Publisher also represents the newspaper within the communities it serves and manages day-to-day operations.

When Gray Communications acquired this newspaper back in 1995 (then called the Post-Tribune), it was published three times a week and reached about 14,000 homes each issue. In just two years, we have grown to daily publication Tuesday through Sunday, averaging paid circulation of 48,900 copies each day.

In March, next year, we will add more than 15,000 more homes served by Genesis Cable, bringing us close to 65,000 copies daily, making us the fifth largest daily in the state.

Explosive growth of such magnitude requires considerable management attention, and since I am also the Publisher of the Rockdale Citizen, it has been difficult for me to maintain an equal presence at both newspapers.

I will continue as president of the company. We've accomplished much in a few short years, but we still have a long way to go. We're encouraged by feedback we've received from readers and advertisers as we strive to produce a quality newspaper that serves the Gwinnett community.

Rick Rae is the president of Post-Citizen Media

CHAPTER THIRTY-THREE

MASTERS MEMORIES

BUDDY PACK....LARGER THAN LIFE

This Masters week I have been remembering Masters of times past.

My first Masters visit was in 1982. I was the newly appointed publisher of the Mountain Press in Sevierville Tennessee. I had arrived in the latter part of 1980 and during much of the following year the pages of our newspaper were full of stories about Shagbark, a development located just outside of Pigeon Forge undertaken by a charismatic entrepreneur named Buddy Pack.

The stories about Shagbark related the troubles that owners were experiencing with accessing their properties due to impassable roads, inadequate land maintenance and other examples of neglect by C.C. Pack, the developer.

Buddy complained loudly about our paper's coverage of these matters, saying we were damaging his business and threatening to sue if we continued to present what he claimed was only one side of the story. Buddy came to my office and invited me to come to Shagbark, drive around the development with him, tour the property and see for myself. I took Buddy up on the offer and spent the better part of a day walking through some of the homes he had built, exploring the terrain and traveling the roads that were muddy but passable but only with a rugged, all-wheel drive or off-road vehicle.

The following week I related the visit to our readers with an article accompanied by some photos that I had taken that presented the development in a generally positive nature. I explained that like any new development in the mountains of East Tennessee some inconvenience was bound to be experienced by residents as access roads were opened, land cleared and new construction completed. Buddy was happy to have his side of the story presented and ultimately became a regular advertiser in our tourist publication reserving the back cover each week for his Shagbark vacation home development.

Over the next several months the dynamic Mr. Pack was in the news more often as he experienced some financial problems relating to his Shagbark property and an adjacent development called Saddle Ridge. We covered these events but always made certain we gave Buddy an opportunity to provide his comments. As 1982 began Buddy was in the news more often as his financial world began to collapse. He failed to meet delinquent payments due his largest lenders and was sued by property owners to whom he sold, claiming they could not gain clear titles to their homes

In March that year Buddy invited me to accompany him to attend the Masters tournament in Augusta, Georgia. I thought it over and decided to accept his invitation. We arranged to meet on Friday morning at Sevier County airport where we boarded Buddy's King Air. In addition to the two pilots there were seven passengers.... Buddy, myself, his attorney, a local judge and three young ladies who acted as attendants and hostesses. As the plane lifted off into a light rain the weather began to deteriorate. By the time we landed in Georgia it had turned into a driving rainstorm.

During the flight Buddy explained that in addition to being a developer, he managed the affairs of professional golfer, J.C. Snead, nephew of Sam Snead who had arranged tickets for us all the gate. Snead, a Tennessee State graduate won 8 times on the PGA tour. By the time we arrived at Augusta National the rain had subsided a little, but it was still overcast. Challenging weather conditions on Thursday and Friday led to the cut at 154 (+10), the highest since the cut was introduced in 1957 and still the highest ever with the co-leaders, Craig Stadler and Curtis Strange, at even par 144.

As we entered the grounds the footing was very risky, and the smell was awful. We learned that the heavy dose of fertilizer that is applied to the grounds resulted in the terrible smell that permeated the place as the walkways turned into sticky, smelly, goo. We all were careful not to get mud on our shoes but that was nearly impossible.... especially for Buddy. Always a fashionable dresser, he was decked out with white golf slacks, matching white golf shirt, white cashmere sweater, matching white socks and white zippered ankle boots.

Disaster struck as we approached the sixth hole. Six is a 180-yard par three that has a steeply elevated tee looking down on the sixteenth green on the right-hand side. The footing around that elevated tee was uncertain, and, as Buddy turned to follow a drive, he lost his footing and began a long slide down the hill that sent up a rooster tail of mud. As everyone looked on in concern, I hustled over to a nearby concession stand and requested a towel. The only towels available were 24 inch green masters golf bag towels at a cost of $39.95 each...but hell I was his guest, so out came my wallet. I spent over two hundred dollars on towels and carefully made my way to Buddy's side and helped to wipe the mud off.

Stadler eventually managed to win the 1982 Masters, but my only memorable moment was of the mud.

After the Masters, Buddy's world really caved in, as his major lenders foreclosed, and he declared bankruptcy. My newspaper even had to place his advertising account in collection.

One day in mid-June Buddy appeared at my office in high spirits. He was now living in Florida and told me he had just closed a deal to develop some Gulf shores property. He was flush with cash and was settling some long-standing debts with people who had helped him in Tennessee. With that he paid me the ten thousand dollars he owed us for his advertising bill and went on his way.

Buddy passed away in in Naples, Florida in 2017.

C. C. 'Buddy' Pack

Rick Rae lives in Loganville and was publisher of the Daily Post and Rockdale Citizen from 1996 to 2007.

CHAPTER THIRTY-FOUR

THE THUNDERBIRD PROJECT

THE RETRO CLASSIC RETURNS

It was the summer of 2002 and I had just seen the newly styled Ford Thunderbird of that year. The car had been designed back in 1999 and was to be launched at the beginning of the new century but various problems at Ford had delayed the launch.

I loved the 'Retro' styling of the new 'Bird which went on sale in the middle of 2002. This marked the eleventh version of the Thunderbird marque which was originally launched in 1955. I fell in love with the styling although I had recently acquired a new 2003 Mitsubishi Spyder and could not consider the T-Bird. Plus, its' sticker price was in the $50,000 area which was well out of my price range.

Since Ford owned the Jaguar brand at that time, the new T-Bird went on the Jaguar chassis and was powered by the Jaguar 3.9 liter engine that developed 280 horsepower, the same engine that powered the Lincoln LS model. They were built at the Wixom, Michigan plant in limited numbers.

As time passed, I watched as the Thunderbird continued to be sold but it was not a raging success. The 2003 model sported a slightly upgraded engine but by 2005 production was discontinued with the release of the 50th golden anniversary edition.

By then I had been scouring used car lots in search of a reasonably priced 2005 model as that was what I wanted. In late 2007, I found a golden anniversary model on a lot in Cleveland, Georgia that had been picked up at auction in Knoxville, Tennessee the week before.

This 'Bird was one of just 552 made in metallic Bronze with a matching light sand leather interior and boasted the matching removable hardtop with 'porthole' windows made famous by the 1957 model T-Bird. I researched the provenance of this car and found that at 552 out of the entire production run out of Wixom of just 8,286 this was a rare 'Bird indeed. It was originally sold to a customer on April 27, 2006 out of Ted Russell Ford in Knoxville.

THUNDERBIRD 55th ANNIVERSARY

Ford World Headquarters - Dearborn, Michigan   June 26, 2010

I became very familiar with the double overhead camshaft engine in this car and made a few modifications to it.... A Borla exhaust system, a Clarion DVD/Navigation/Sound system, 17-inch chrome wheels with 245/55 Diamondback wide whitewalls and K & N cold air intake system. The engine put out 305 horsepower and showed 281.6 rear wheel horsepower on the dynamometer.

The DOHC Jaguar engine in the T-Bird was very hard on Coil packs or as I came to know them, "COPS". The T-Bird did not have a traditional coil, using instead, an electrical device called "Coil On Plug" with each spark plug having its own power source. These little devils were prone to failure due to excessive heat or moisture and were extremely difficult to replace. Each pack was held in place by a 7/16" hex nut that was well hidden and to replace a failed pack on either the number 4 or number 8 cylinder (back of the engine close to the firewall, under the cowl) was a nightmare. In order to access this nut, I manufactured a 7/16" box end spanner using a torch to heat up the tool so I could bend it on the proper angle to get up into that COPS retainer. The tight space allowed a quarter turn of the wrench at a time. To replace all eight of them the dealer charged $800 labor. To do it myself took me two hours. Each pack itself cost $6.95.

Owners were always in dread of that mild throttle hesitation that indicated a COPS was on its way out. Some of them failed after 5,000 miles, others at 10,000 and some never failed. Of course, cylinders 4 and 8 were usually in the hottest area where moisture accumulated and those were the first to fail. When one failed the car would go into limp mode, limiting your speed to 45 mph.

In April of 2010 I got an invitation from the Ford Motor Company to come to Dearborn and attend a celebration of the 55th birthday of the Thunderbird. Some owners of the rarest Thunderbirds were asked to bring their cars home to Dearborn and join in a week of partying, parades and fun with fellow owners and Ford executives, including their new president, Alan Mulally.

So, in June of 2010 I travelled to the famous Ford Glass House, partied with many folks, paraded around Greenfield Village, raced my car around the test track at the Ford Proving Grounds and had a wonderful time all at Ford's expense. (they even paid for my gasoline!). I put over 35,000 miles on that Thunderbird including a trip to a car show in Ottawa, Canada where my car won five awards.

In August of 2010 I sold my 'Bird to a lady in South Carolina for $4,000 more than I paid for it. This marked one of the few times in my life that I ever made money on a car.

Rick Rae is president of Post Citizen Media.

CHAPTER THIRTY-FIVE

JUST A LITTLE DIFFERENT

By Rick Rae
Publisher

One of the things we dread most around The Mountain Press is covering check presentations. Usually, we get a call about an organization donating funds to some worthy cause and they ask that we cover the event.

Unfortunately, there really isn't any "event" to cover. While we certainly feel that the donation of money to worthy causes is a good thing, we also know from experience that pictures of two or three people staring at the camera while passing a check from one to the other are dry, uninteresting and boring.

Some organizations have tried to get around this by making their checks 10 feet wide, or writing them on shirt backs or pieces of plywood. Those techniques have been used so often that they too, are old hat.

When we go to cover check presentations we try to get creative with our photos. We would much rather picture what the money will do or is doing and get some action into the photo, but that's not always easy.

Last week we had that challenge again when the Sevier Medical Center Auxiliary called to tell me they had the first check against their pledge to the Sevier Medical Center capital fund campaign ready to go. As chairman of the family gifts division for the campaign, I was destined to be pictured in yet another boring shot.

John Fox was assigned to take the photo and it was John's idea to get creative and try to show a bit of what donations such as the auxiliary's really do. Consequently, we took the photo in the operating room beside the equipment that donations such as this are used to buy. Since the operating room is sterile and needs to be kept that way, we all had to put on "clean greens" to keep the room protected. That made the photo even more interesting.

Even John had to dress up and although a photo of John would not normally be published, I couldn't resist the opportunity to share it here.

From left: Auxiliary president Mary Jane Goodpaster, Rick Rae and John Fox.

The challenge is there to all groups and organizations who want publicity about presentations of checks and other items. Help us make the shots interesting. The dry, fixed smile shots of a check changing hands needs to be phased out and we'll welcome your suggestions on how to make that happen.

CHAPTER THIRTY-SIX

One day in 1987 I took a shot at defining what news means to our readers.

WHAT'S NEWS?

How does one decide what is advertising and what is news?

That question has been raised several times this past week and I'm afraid that my response to the folks involved wasn't as clear as it should have been.

We had a couple of instances where we tried to use our news judgment on items submitted to us and decided that since they failed the news definition, the items would have to be considered as paid advertising. In retrospect, we probably judged too harshly as there may have been some news value, but it is a very tough decision.

As a general rule, if an item submitted to us for publication will have appeal to a large segment of our reading audience (in our opinion), we will edit it to our style and format and publish it as news. Included in this category are weddings, engagements, first birthdays, obituaries, silver and golden wedding anniversaries, or other significant events such as graduations, military advancement, etcetera.

If you want your third anniversary noted in the paper, worded exactly as you've written, with the picture printed an exact size, the item now becomes an advertisement and we'll be happy to publish it as paid space.

Between these two examples, there are some problems, however. What if two sets of twins are married to each other and are celebrating a 10th anniversary? Is that newsworthy? What if three couples were all married on the same day and are celebrating their 15th together? Is that newsworthy? This is where we try to exercise judgment and sometimes our judgment is in error.

Of course, judgment can be influenced sometimes by the approach. If a person asks for an item to be considered as a news story, providing a reasonable explanation as to why it may be of interest to many of our readers, we'll probably be more inclined to consider it than one from someone who tells us what to say, how to display it, when to print it and where it should be positioned in the paper. Sometimes it all boils down to human relations.

Another area that gives us fits comes under the heading of community service. If a service club or organization is trying to raise money for a worthy cause, how much space can we devote to help them? In the past we have written articles to help publicize such items and we've even donated space for ongoing programs if the organization is community-wide such as the United Way.

But what if a group wants us to run an item showcasing donors to their cause every time a significant contribution is made? How do we react to those requests? Right now, for example we're in the middle of a fund raising campaign for the hospital expansion; several churches are involved in fund raisers; Sevier County, Gatlinburg-Pittman and Seymour schools are all trying to raise money for everything from sports activities to band uniforms; the Dennis Mize tournament organizers are trying to raise money to support junior golf; one of our local service clubs is organizing a road race to raise money for community projects, another uses a pancake breakfast, while another organizes a craft fair.

Do we open our news columns to help these folks in their causes?

Of course, we do, but there are some limitations.

We'll give any worthwhile cause news coverage. We may even publish more than one item but it would have to be a very significant event. It seems that this county has more non-profit groups attempting to raise funds than most I've seen and each feel that their project is the most important one in the county. That's the way it should be.

If we seem a bit fatigued when asked to publicize the arts council, little theatre, the cultural center, the rescue squad, band boosters, athletic support groups, the animal shelter, PTA functions, swim teams, school clubs, and various and sundry other very worthwhile organizations; please pardon us.

We only have so much space, so much time and so much patience. Those who request support usually are much happier with the result than those who demand it.

Rick Rae is publisher of the Mountain Press.

CHAPTER THIRTY-SEVEN

DON'T PUT A LABEL ON US

By Rick Rae
Publisher

This column is being written prior to the Nov. 4 election but it will not be published until the results are in.

Right now, I have no idea who the next governor of the state will be and based on what I have seen and heard during the course of the campaign, I'm not at all sure I even care.

Both candidates have visited our offices, both have talked with our editor, both have run advertisements in this newspaper, but we deliberately refrained from endorsing either one.

That inaction came as quite a shock to some in Sevier County. There are those we count among our good friends who couldn't believe we wouldn't endorse the Republican candidate for Governor. After all, isn't The Mountain Press a Republican newspaper?

Let's dispel that one first.

We are not a Republican newspaper. We are not a Democratic newspaper either.

We are a Sevier County newspaper.

If that were to mean that we felt a Democrat would do the best job of representing the interests of Sevier County, we would probably endorse that person, despite the fact that over 90 percent of the population in this county votes Republican.

A two-party system is one of the things that made America strong and if there are folks out there who feel one party is all we need, regardless of who runs on the ticket and what the platform, I'd suggest they may be in the wrong country.

As a Sevier County newspaper, we feel that one of our roles is to try and reflect the mood and feeling of the community. That doesn't mean that we have to follow blindly what went on before.

One of the forerunners of the newspaper was called the Record-Republican and in prior years the paper spoke with a decided Republican voice. Even under the leadership of Bill Postlewaite, our stance was unquestionably Republican.

Today, there are a few newspapers continuing to lean along party lines but for the most part they follow the candidate, regardless of party affiliation. They are more concerned about communicating information than in shaping opinion unless they feel very strongly about an issue. That is an apt description of the way we operate.

The same is true of our other Harte-Hanks newspapers in New England, South Carolina, Georgia, Arkansas, Texas and California. None that I know of has any strong political affiliation.

As regular readers know, we operate with an editorial board and all three must agree before we publish an opinion. In the case of the gubernatorial race there wasn't much discussion. The Democratic candidate got one member reasonably enthused and the Republican platforms raised the interest of another. By and large, however, there wasn't enough interest in the campaign to generate an endorsement for either.

My personal observation is that there appeared to be more energy spent in tearing down the reputation and qualifications of each other than in genuinely communicating what planned to carry out during his term of office.

Perhaps that is why neither candidate looked particularly appetizing to us. By this time, that will all be academic anyway.

CHAPTER THIRTY-EIGHT

A NEW PERSPECTIVE

SURVIVING RMSF

This column was published after a lengthy stay in the hospital and made me thankful to be alive.

A new perspective

This week I will celebrate another birthday. Which one it is becomes quite insignificant at my age. Suffice to say, I am past what we used to call retirement age - before the cost of gasoline and taxes went up and the retirement plans and long-term investments went down.

What is significant is the fact that I will be celebrating the anniversary at all. A year ago I was literally on my deathbed in the hospital.

Five doctors had gathered 'round, unable to diagnose what was ailing me, and one of them had informed my wife that she should keep the family close at hand as *"it didn't look good"*

Miraculously, Dr. Tzvetan Vassilev, a specialist in infectious diseases, happened to ask my wife if an insect had bitten me recently. When she mentioned that I had complained about a tick bite 10 days prior to that while we were vacationing in Yellowstone, "bingo," the light went on! He immediately began treatment for a disease in the Rickettsia family, related to typhoid fever, called Rocky Mountain spotted fever. About 20 percent of the 215 people in North America who were infected with this disease last year died because it is so hard to diagnose. I'm glad I was an 80 percenter.

A year later, I am left with kidneys that aren't quite as strong as they were, a blood condition that is under treatment, an arrhythmia, or irregular heartbeat, that I didn't have before and the lingering effects of a short-term memory loss because of the extremely high fever that tried hard to fry my brain. Most of my memory loss returned within a couple of months, but sometimes I have to work hard to bring back a person's name, a place, a song or a number, whereas they came to me quite quickly before I got sick.

What I am also left with is a greater appreciation for life, for friends and for family. There is a line in a Jimi Hendrix song called "Look to Your Soul" that goes "to really live you must almost die," and I know now what that means.

Today, I count my blessings each morning and every night. Simple things, like enjoying a meal, laughing with co-workers, competing with friends on the golf course, riding in the woods or just listening to music mean much more to me now. I feel I am closer to God just riding with my horse through the trails than ever before.

Interestingly, I think I am less serious about things than before. The health and growth of the newspaper is important, but it will be around long after I am not.

There is clean air to breathe. Flowers to smell. Good food to taste. There are places I have not yet visited. Friends I have yet to meet. Old friends I need to revisit, birdies I have yet to score and trails I have yet to ride.

Life is sweet; don't take it for granted.

Rick Rae is a vice president of Triple Crown Media and publisher of the Rockdale Citizen and Gwinnett Daily Post in Georgia. From 1979 to 1986, he was publisher of The Mountain Press.

CHAPTER THIRTY-NINE

NO ROOM FOR MARGINAL WORK

By Rick Rae
Publisher

The paper has been full of news lately about how local governments, city and county, are in need of increased funds to handle their fiscal obligations.

Increases in property taxes and/or sales taxes are apparently required to offset reductions in federal money available and to fund the ever-increasing costs of operations.

All this is understandable and makes sense to me because it is the type of thing that all businesses must go through on a regular basis. In the monetary sense, government is a business. Money is raised through taxes or charges for services and based on the projections of money available and a list of money needed to fund ongoing programs, a budget is prepared to operate against.

One of the largest expense areas in all government budgets, if not the largest, is labor. Personnel costs for the city of Sevierville, for example, in 1986 will total $1,644,800. In Pigeon Forge, the total will be $1.5 million. For Gatlinburg, the cost is $2.6 million.

A ballpark number for all costs associated with personnel funded by our tax dollars in the county, then, is around $5.7 million.

With that in mind maybe the administrators need to be looking harder at just what they're getting for the dollars spent. Are the right people in the right jobs? Are marginal employees allowed to linger on the payroll year after year? Does every employee have a clear understanding of what his or her job really is? Are some jobs being paid at a level that is too high when compared to similar jobs in other departments, or other organizations?

One exercise that may be worth going through is to ask various department heads to assume they have just fired every person in their department. Then ask them to list the order in which they would hire them back to work. In other words, which person would be the last hired back and why? In every department there will be a "last hired." That will probably be the most marginal person in each department. The next step is to find out why the person is marginal and what can be done about it.

Does the employee need counseling? Special training? What can be done to remove them from the marginal list? Once that is established, work should be done to achieve that end. That is the supervisor's responsibility.

Then, within 90 days that employee should either be removed from the marginal list or removed from the organization. The employee should be told exactly what is expected of them, what standard needs to be met and how long they have to meet it. Feedback on how the employee is progressing will lead the supervisor and the employee to the obvious conclusion. "We either give the taxpayer full value for their money, or we stop wasting it by finding someone who can."

Marginal employees can really multiply labor costs. Not only is the money paid on them being wasted, but other employees usually have to take up the slack, which makes them less productive as a result.

Another problem is morale. It's an accepted premise that when morale is high, people can accomplish more and are happier, more productive employees. Conversely, when morale is low, production slips.

The most damaging thing to high morale is to work in an organization that condones marginal performance or attitude. How can you expect a person always to give their best when they know that a co-worker is allowed to slack off, undermine the department or not pull their share of the load?

This is a continuing challenge that businesses face every day. As a taxpayer, I would hope that our local governments will operate in the same manner.

CHAPTER FORTY

At the time I was publisher of the Mountain Press in East
Tennessee a virtual war was being raised between long-time
residents who wanted parts of the county to remain 'dry' with
no alcoholic beverages being sold within those confines.

As a county newcomer who sometimes enjoyed to have
a beer with my pizza, I agreed with tourists who would
complain to our newspaper about the absence of alcoholic
drinks at local restaurants. *"How can you claim to be
a primary tourist destination"*, they complained, *if we
can't enjoy a beverage of our choice with a meal?"*

Our paper took a stance in support of legalization
and I even volunteered to write some advertisements
to help out the local tourism council. That generated
a lot of heat from local bootleggers as well as local
religious leaders. Finally, I wrote this column.

TIME TO FACE REALITIES

By RICK RAE
Publisher

The ostrich was surrounded. There was adversity on every side. As the enemy closed in, the ostrich buried his head in the sand, thinking that if he could not see them, his enemies would go away. He never knew what hit him.

Sevier County is getting to be a great place to look for ostriches.

In Gatlinburg, they remember the sleepy mountain town of old and some refuse to look at the problems of today. A pleasant stroll down the Parkway has become akin to running the gauntlet. Street vendors and peddlers of typical tourist trap junk are turning Gatlinburg into what they used to accuse Pigeon Forge of being. Some action is being taken, but let's hope that the ostriches don't outnumber those that are doing something worthwhile.

The county court is a good place to hunt for ostriches. While it's true that not all of our problems can be solved with money alone, we can't bury our heads to the monetary problems the county will face in the coming years. Why not a sales tax increase AND a property tax increase to start building for the future, instead of a patchwork plan for today.

Some feel that Pigeon Forge has a good-sized ostrich population as well. A great many citizens of this community want to eliminate beer entirely and forgo any tax revenues associated with its sale.

The people opposed to the sale of beer and alcohol have beliefs that are important to them. Those who hold those views need to ask if it is possible to achieve their goal through legislation, however.

Beer purchased outside city limits just 200 yards up Wears Valley Road, or beer purchased in Gatlinburg or Knoxville could be just as harmful as beer purchased in Pigeon Forge.

History has shown us in lesson after lesson that things just cannot be legislated out of existence. Beer, like liquor, guns, knives and automobiles can cause serious injury if misused, of that there is no doubt. Trying to legislate it away, however, may have the opposite effect.

Prohibition did not work. The eighteenth amendment calling for the prohibition of intoxicating liquors was passed by congress on December 18, 1917. Sixteen years later it was repealed in the wake of increased alcoholism and alcohol abuse.

Why?

Perhaps for the same reason that women, deprived of the right to vote, fought like the devil to obtain it. Why people who were denied religious freedom fought tooth and nail to keep it. Why blacks, deprived of civil rights, fought with fury to gain them. Time and time again, history has taught that the best way to motivate is to try and deprive.

It's interesting that the only two alcoholics that I have ever been personally associated with (an ex-employee and an ex-neighbor) were both raised in homes where alcohol was never permitted.

Perhaps those opposed to the sale of beer should recognize the wisdom of those councilmen who have voted for the measure. Particularly those who share their beliefs. Those councilmen know the lessons of history and are to be commended for keeping cool heads under fire.

Beer itself is not an enemy. Lack of education as to its danger and ease of misuse is. We cannot abolish beer but we can use the tax revenues from its sale to educate.

Elimination or education, which is more realistic?

CHAPTER FORTY-ONE

NEWS, EDITORIALS, COLUMNS AND OPINIONS: DIFFERENCES

By Rick Rae
Publisher

I hope that I've conveyed some sense of how we go about this business of publishing a newspaper over the past several weeks. Today, I'd like to delve into the differences between "fact" and "opinion".

At the top of this page you'll see the dictionary definition of opinion. It's there because of a discussion I had a couple of years ago with a reader who told me he felt that our paper was biased and that our opinions were too one-sided. When I asked him if he knew what the definition of an opinion was it became clear he was confusing facts and opinions.

The best explanation of the subject that I've seen was written by our old editor, Butch Walker, a few years back. It's a bit out of date as far as some things he refers to are concerned, but it's interesting to note that his reference to the $2 tax rate is still relevant. (There's an opinion in there folks, but it's between the lines.) Since Butch says it so well, we'll just repeat his column here:

'Your opinion' counts most
By Butch Walker
Editor

There aren't many hard and fast rules in the news business. Though the packages may be similar in appearance, the content of our news product is manufactured from scratch for every issue. The information comes in, and then we make on-the-spot decisions under deadline pressure about what goes where three times a week.

You've got to be flexible, for relativity is everything. You do one thing today, another tomorrow. A story planned for the front page may have to be bumped to the inside of the paper because something more interesting or important has developed.

But we don't entirely play it fast and loose. We follow the basic standards of ethical journalism that have evolved over the years, and we have established some policies to which each member of the editorial staff is expected to adhere.

For a newspaper to command the respect of its community, it must project a sense of fair play, and yet be willing to "take a stand" for the good of the community. Sometimes these basic principles are in conflict with one another. How can we give fair and equal coverage to both sides of a controversial issue and yet still "take a stand?"

As National Newspaper Week comes to a close, your old editor is going to delve into the tricky areas of "fact" and "opinion" with this list of thoughts.

1. Sevier County has a tax rate of $2. That is a fact.
2. Whether a $2 tax rate is bad or good, is a matter of opinion.
3. If a county commissioner says the tax rate is good, that is his opinion. If the commissioner states this view in public or to our reporter, it becomes a **fact** that this commissioner holds a certain **opinion**.
4. If another commissioner says the tax rate is bad, then for a newspaper to **factually report on the issue, both opinions** must be printed.

That's what our news pages are all about. We report facts, and we factually report the properly attributed opinions of others as long as they are not libelous, keeping in mind a sense of fair play to all sides of an issue.

But what about "our opinion," "your opinion," and "my opinion?" That's what the page you are reading now is all about:

- **Our opinion**. This is where we take a stand on the issues. We offer our reasoned judgments as to proper courses of actions which we believe will benefit the community. When you see an editorial labeled "our opinion" it represents the consensus of *The Mountain Press* editorial board which is composed of Rick Rae, publisher; Rick Holmes, county news editor; and your old editor, Butch Walker.

- **My opinion**. You are reading my opinion now. Although it is a matter of semantics, the articles labeled "Editor's notes", "Going my way" by John Fox and "Inside Outlook" by Rick Holmes are not **editorials**; they are **columns**. Other members of the news staff occasionally contribute to this page, and these are labeled "Staff writer's opinion." Rick Rae writes for this page also and his offerings are labeled "Publisher's comments." Opinions stated on this page which carry the writer's byline are individual views.

- **Your opinion**. In my opinion, your opinions as expressed in letters to the editor are the most important reports that our newspapers carry. I'm most proud that over the 2½ years of which I've been your editor, there has been a dramatic increase in letters to the editor. This page has become a public forum open to all who want to express their views. Keep those cards and letters coming, folks.

CHAPTER FORTY-TWO

PRESS: MORE THAN A NAME

By RICK RAE
Publisher

In an earlier column I wrote about one of my recent learning experiences in gaining my high school diploma. Another recent learning experience was devoting some time to learn a bit about operating the presses that this newspaper is printed on.

I decided to spend some time working with the press crew in order to find out more about the inner workings of that sometimes, mysterious piece of equipment.

Thursday afternoon, I reported to Tim Webb, Mountain Press printing manager, for duty. As I joined up with our pressmen in preparing for the printing of the Friday paper I felt a little out of place. Larry McClure literally runs from one side of the press room to the other as he attends to the many tasks of setting up for the run.

Billy Matthews goes about his duties in such a quiet, competent manner that you don't realize how quickly he moves about.

Gene Ownby doesn't say much but he always appears at the right time in the right place to carry out his part of the routine in making things come out properly.

My coming on the scene was a bit like tossing a monkey wrench in the middle of a finely tuned machine. Nonetheless, they put up with my ignorance and stood by patiently as I fumbled around with such tasks as removing printing plates from the cylinders in preparation for the new ones.

They didn't laugh out loud as I botched up the job of locking the new plates in place and they didn't even snicker as I smeared myself with printer's ink while trying to replace the sock on a bottom roller.

The next task was loading the rolls of newsprint onto the roll stands and webbing the units with one, long, continuous sheet of newsprint. The rolls weight about a thousand pounds each and they are swung into position with the help of an electric hoist. We try to keep wasted or damaged newsprint to a minimum since the cost is so high and it is a very delicate job to make the roll drop into the right place without having hit the sides of the stands.

My first attempt went OK, so I got a bit cocky with the second one and watched in humiliation as about 40 feet of newsprint got stripped off as waste. Each roll must have a heavy steel shaft locked in place secured by a locking collar and after taking these out and putting them in a few times, I realized one of the reasons that the forearms and biceps of Tim, Larry, Billy and Gene are bigger than mine.

Once the plates and rolls are in place the units are powered up and the press is inched along in order to position the pages in the proper place on the sheet. At this time the cutoff and color registration is set, prior to running the presses up to speed.

Once that task is complete the power to the two 50-horsepower motors is increased and a heavy roar signifies that the press run is under way. As papers begin to run out the conveyor, the press room is a flurry of activity as ink density is adjusted, tension is set and registration is fine-tuned.

From then on the press must be kept fed with its two main ingredients of paper and ink. Black ink is pumped into ink fountains directly from an ink tank, but it still must be spread by hand evenly in the fountain. Colored ink is hand dipped from buckets to the fountains and that can get messy if you're clumsy like me.

Ink is thick and gooey, almost like vaseline, but you have to move quickly with it or it slops over everything. As I was scooping a thick blob of green into the fountain it jumped right off the spatula and onto the rollers. I watched in horror as it spread over the unit and looked up as Tim came running back to see why the newspapers coming out at his end had a big smear in the middle of the page. If any of those papers got out and you received one, please accept my apologies.

The next day I learned a bit more about the operation and got pretty good at crimping plates and locking them on the press. I also kept the ink fountains full without getting ink all over me or the press. They even let me handle the controls that slow it down and start it up.

By Saturday, I felt I had a good understanding of how the paper is printed, but it would take months, or even years to become an expert at the job. Through it all the fact that we have some very dedicated employees was reinforced.

The lesson learned is that you should never take any task for granted. If you operate a business, it makes good sense to get familiar with every part of it.

CHAPTER FORTY-THREE

This was the last column I wrote that appeared in the Georgia Newspapers that I had published for eleven years. It ran on June 28, 2006.

MOMENTOUS DAYS AHEAD

REFLECTIONS OF THE PAST AND A LOOK TO THE FUTURE

The final week of June will mark a few significant events in my life.

Thursday, I will celebrate my 67th birthday, which is pretty amazing. For many years I thought that I would never live past the age of fifty-one; that was my father's age when he passed away. Thankfully, I am in good health, possess lots of energy and my golf handicap is holding at thirteen.

It is noteworthy that I have lived in eight decades (just caught a bit of the thirties) and, although I love the past I think this decade is my favorite so far.

On Friday, Penny and I will celebrate 44 years of marriage, and that is also amazing. That she has put up with me for that length of time is more a testimony to her patience and understanding that to anything I have contributed to the union. What seems unusual today is that our kids have the same set of parents that they started out with.

Also, on Friday, I will be officially retiring from our newspaper group. Just about eleven years ago I moved to Georgia to take on the task of publishing the Rockdale Citizen and the Gwinnett Daily Post. Much has happened in that time.

Back then, the Citizen was only published five days a week with circulation of less than 10,000 in Rockdale County. Today, the two Citizen newspapers serve Rockdale and Newton counties and reach a total of 16,000 homes, seven days a week.

In Gwinnett the Daily Post was a struggling 13,000 daily, and today it boasts of 63,000 circulation on weekdays and 104,000 on Sunday, making it the second largest Sunday paper in the state! Watching these papers grow has been a pleasurable part of my career.

Many of my co-workers were here when I first came on the scene and over the years they have become friends as well. People like Alice Queen, Brenda Bennett, Bill Herbert, Barbara Knowles, Denise Clay, Howard Reed and Susan Andrews learned to tolerate my bad habits, made fun of my Canadian accent and became part of our extended family.

On July 1, I will be starting a new venture. My new company, Rae Media Services will be taking on clients in need of services consulting on marketing, advertising, production or acquisition analysis. Additionally, we are negotiating to acquire one of the largest color comic distributors in the southeast and, I have already signed one long-term deal with the folks who own these newspapers. While I won't be around as much, I'll still have a hand in some of their continued development.

The Daily Post is in the capable hands of J.K. Murphy. Back when I was publisher of the Daily Post in November, 1998, I recruited J.K. from Indiana to join us as editor of the Gwinnett paper. We promoted him to publisher last fall and he and the newspaper have a great future in front of them.

The Rockdale and Newton papers are now overseen by Alice Queen, who sits in the publisher's chair. When I came on the scene in early 1996 the Citizen had no editor, but Alice was the person holding things together in the newsroom after the paper had gone through some traumatic changes.

My first appointment was to elevate her to editor, and soon the paper regained the kind of news gathering reputation it had earned under the tutelage of Tom Barry and Fred Turner. A short time later Alice convinced me that Newton County could support a daily newspaper and was instrumental in launching the Newton Citizen that now has circulation of nearly 7,500 each day.

Another big part of our newspaper operation is the Albany Herald. Just this past year, Mike Gebhart was promoted from general manager to publisher there, and he has been keeping things running at an even keel at our operations at the southern end of the state.

Over the past several months, I've had the pleasure of welcoming Bonnie Pratt into our Atlanta area newspaper family. As group publisher, Bonnie heads up operations at the Clayton News-Daily, Henry Daily Herald and the Jackson Progress-Argus.

I'm excited about the future of our company and its seven newspapers. Hopefully I can help this number grow.

Rick Rae is a vice president of Triple Crown Media. On July 1 he will become president of Rae Media Services Inc. and chairman of Continental Features.

(30)

ABOUT THE AUTHOR

Richard Rae was born and educated in Hamilton, Canada. He dropped out of high school in 1957 without graduating. After a short stint working as a bank teller, he joined International Harvester Company in his hometown of Hamilton, Canada as a clerk. He was promoted to the diesel truck division as a specification writer and then on to writing owners and operators manuals for other international products.

After five years at Harvester, he moved to London, Ontario to become an advertising copywriter for Western Tire and Auto Supply, a company with sixty stores located throughout Canada's eastern provinces.

His first book was written in 2011 and begins with his return to his hometown to begin work in a newspaper career that spanned forty-four years. Rae and his family immigrated to the United States in 1973 to Michigan where he joined Capital Cities Corporation as retail advertising manager at the *Oakland Press.*

He became a United States citizen in 1982 after being promoted to the position of Publisher of the Mountain Press in east Tennessee. He continued his education and graduated from high school that same year. For most of his newspaper career he has worked in public companies such as Southam Newspapers, Capital Cities Corporation, Harte-Hanks Communications, Gray Television and Triple Crown Media.

Career side trips with Worrell Enterprises, Sutherland Newspapers, Southern Farm Publications, Ogden Newspapers, Tribune Review Printing and Chatfield-Taylor Corporation have helped round out his experience. While short on scholastic education, Rick has loads of practical knowledge gained in his travels as a manager of publications in four Canadian Cities and Ten American States.

For the last eleven years of his career, Rick managed newspapers in the Suburban Atlanta area, first as publisher of the Gwinnett Daily Post and Rockdale Citizen and then as president of Post Citizen Media. When Gray Television spun off those properties into a new public entity called Triple Crown Media, Rick became a vice president, overseeing operations of the Gwinnett and Rockdale newspapers as well as the Newton Citizen, the Clayton News Daily, the Henry Herald and the Jackson Progress Argus.

In 2006, Rae retired from Triple Crown after he and his wife formed Rae Media Services Incorporated and bought Continental Features, a provider of color comics to Sunday newspapers in the southeastern USA. After managing that company for twelve years he retired for a second time in 2018. At age 83, Rick and his wife, Penny enjoy their retirement in Loganville, Georgia.

KEEP READING FOR A REVIEW OF RICK RAE'S EARLIER BOOK

Not Extinct Yet from *Editor and Publisher Magazine*

If you're more than 50 years old you will either think this story was coincidently familiar to your own unpredictable publishing odyssey, or immediately upon finishing "Not Extinct Yet", you're going to call FTD and order Rick Rae and his wife a Sympathy bouquet.

If you're younger than 50 you will not only be entertained chapter by chapter, but you will gain valuable insight and street smarts on how to confront and solve publishing's many obstacles.

Fifty-four years in the newspaper business is equivalent to 308 years in a 'normal' career. Somehow, Rae was able to condense his adventure into 170 pages, but it has the same fast, energizing, emotional, fun ride of Six Flag's Ultra Twister-- during a 7.1 magnitude earthquake.

Just when you think Rae's settled into a stable position and ready to move smoothly forward, a G-Force, "you've got to be kidding" spiral turns you upside down and rockets into another chapter.

From embezzling employees, Dolly Parton's big heart, Australian Sharks, a devastating fire, and a publisher obsessed with porn, readers should strap themselves in before settling down to read this book.

Don't be fooled by the title, "Not Extinct Yet" reflects the writer's perseverance more than it describes the spellbinding journey. A better title might have been "Forty-Four years on a Nonstop Roller-Coaster."-*JF*

Not Extinct Yet is available in paperback, hard cover or electronic version from....

www.authorhouse.com/en/bookstore or call 833.262.8899

Printed in the United States
by Baker & Taylor Publisher Services